ALMOST EVERYTHING YOU WANTED TO KNOW ABOUT TICKLING

ALMOST EVERYTHING YOU WANTED TO KNOW ABOUT TICKLING

AN INTERNATIONAL STUDY

Duncan Taub

ALMOST EVERYTHING YOU WANTED TO KNOW ABOUT TICKLING
An International Study

Edited by Lana Kisner

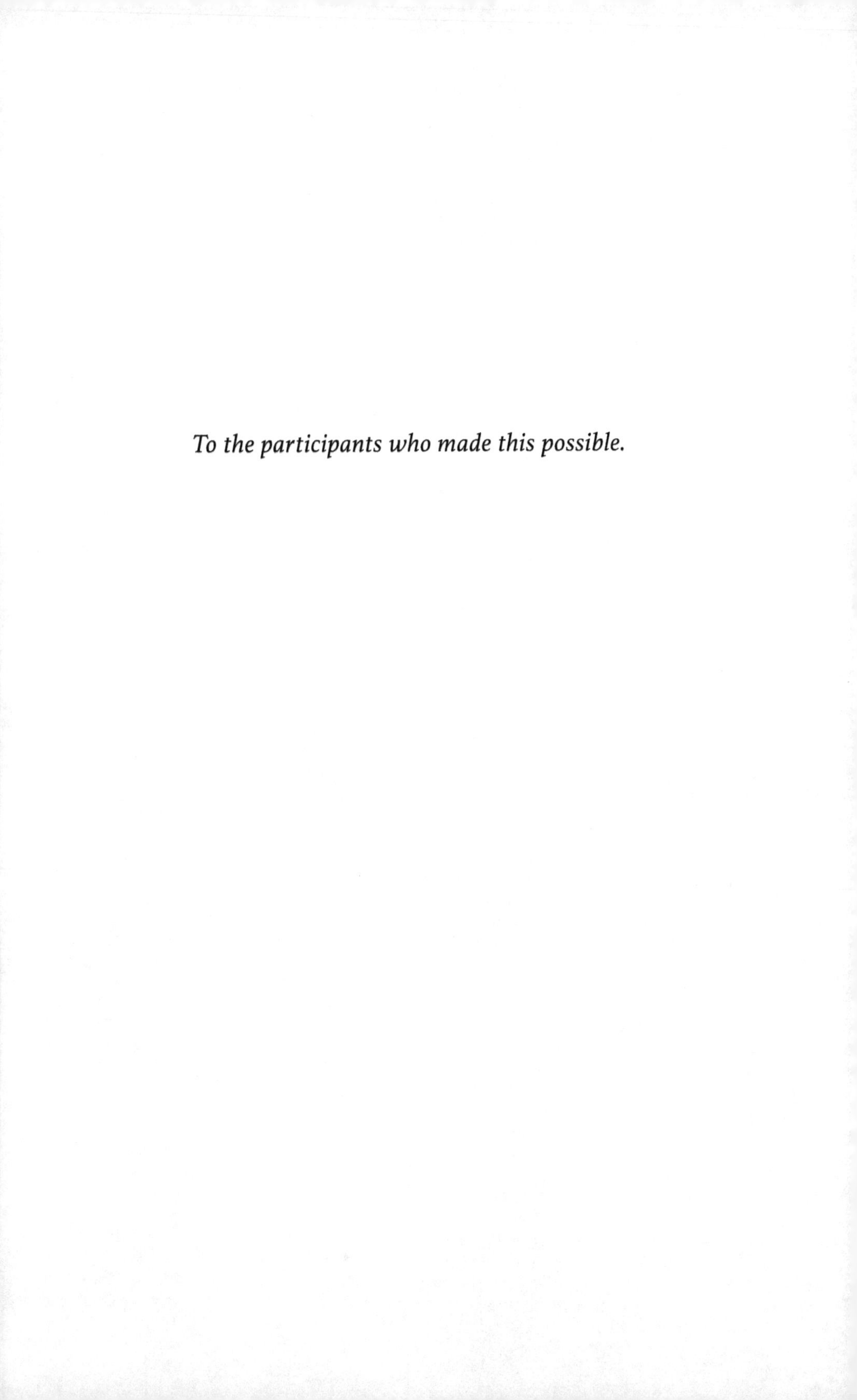

To the participants who made this possible.

TABLE OF CONTENTS

INTRODUCTION

We'll begin by showing our arrogance, a surefire method to win you over. Here it goes. "You have never read a book similar to this one." How could we possibly say this? There must be tons of research about tickling. Not true. There's not much research of any kind and certainly no international study of the social role that tickling plays. Those setting the research agenda believe that tickling is a weird, useless behavior that is unimportant, uninteresting, and already understood well enough to meet anyone's needs. They're wrong.

TICKLING RESEARCH IS IMPORTANT

The prime example of an important topic for research is the human brain. Our brain is amazing. Other animals have wonderful brains, but the human version is a class apart.

Another feature that sets us apart from all other animals is ticklishness. Tickling exists in other animals, but they are much less ticklish and have far fewer reasons for tickling. The same conditions during our evolution that led to what many believe is the most marvelous creation in the universe (the human brain) also led to this other complex creation, human ticklishness. This is not to imply that ticklishness is on the same level as the human brain. (We may be fanatic about our research, but we are not crazy.) It does imply, however, that evolution went to a lot of trouble designing a specific ticklishness that separates humans from all other animals, and evolution don't make no junk.

If it's not junk, then what's it around for? How common is it? How does it affect us? What's it good for? How is it misused? Are we stuck with something that helped our species 100,000 years ago, but is now just a nuisance? This book does not provide definitive answers to any of these questions, but it gives interesting insights that advance our understanding.

TICKLING RESEARCH IS INTERESTING
It's interesting because it's weird.

1. Lightly touching a particular place on a particular person can send them into spasms of laughter.
2. Possible responses to tickles range from total loss of control to no response at all; from sensitive feet and insensitive bellies to the reverse; and from overwhelming discomfort to mind-blowing orgasm.
3. For some, tickling is more intimate than sex; and for others, it's just fun with friends.
4. Sensations from tickling can be enjoyable, energizing, exciting, relaxing, sexual, painful, itchy, enraging, or the same as any other touch. What makes it even weirder is that these different, apparently contradictory sensations can occur in

the same person at different places on the body, at different times in the same places, or even simultaneously.

Are there any other sensations that make less sense?

TICKLING RESEARCH IS INADEQUATE

Tickling has icky parts; it may make us feel bad or act ridiculously. On top of that, it's usually a boy-girl thing, and boy-girl things have an uncomfortable relationship with respectability. Science handles icky topics the way we all do — by pretending they don't exist. Even if a scientist was willing to risk her career to study an icky topic, she couldn't do it because she would need funding, and there is no National Institute for Icky Topics.

We claim that this is the first large-scale, in-depth, international study of tickling. Almost always in science, it is wrong and arrogant to claim to be the first. In this case, however, the claim is probably correct and certainly not arrogant. The reasons similar studies were not done previously had nothing to do with the expertise or creativity of the scientists. It was solely because tickling research does not advance scientific careers or help secure grants, the driving forces for research.

These reasons, however, were not barriers for a retired researcher. With the resources that have recently been made available on the internet, neither was the cost, which would have been prohibitive until the internet provided easy access to freelancers across the world.

This study is only the beginning of population-based research on tickling; no questions were, or even could have been, answered definitively. However, in all immodesty, it is not a bad beginning, especially for a self-financed study conducted without institutional support. The study is certainly good enough to provide a baseline for comparison and guidance to future studies. And many results that were especially strong in this study will probably hold up in later studies.

DESCRIPTION OF OUR STUDY

This study did not evaluate what causes people to be ticklish, why tickling causes laughter, and why some spots on the body are more ticklish than others. That was not our expertise nor our interest. Our interest was to gain a better understanding of the role of tickling in our social lives. To do that, we studied more than 2,000 women from more than 17 countries. These women answered broad-ranging questions that helped us understand the good and bad effects of tickling on their lives and the factors that influenced these effects. We obtained information about how ticklishness varied in the population, the circumstances in which women were tickled, the attitudes and responses of the women to tickling, and the effects of culture, age, relationship status, and personality on their attitudes and responses.

Our findings suggest how the value of tickling for survival and reproduction may have caused ticklishness to evolve, and what value tickling might have today.

HOW TO READ THE BOOK

For those of you interested in how scientists make sausages, we have an appendix that provides background about who was in the study and how the study was done. If sausages are not your thing, you can ignore the appendix without missing any findings from the study.

Some aspects of this book will be strange to you. One of these is the large number of tables, which are loved by scientists but not many others. Please understand that we did not want to do this to you. Unfortunately, replacing tables with words made for a boring mess, and we had to put the tables back. Anyone who by the end of the book considers the tables helpful is welcome to thank us.

To reduce your table trauma, we summarized the most important results before showing you each table. Then you can skip the table guilt-free. More details will be in the tables for those who are interested.

Although this book is based on a scientific study, it is not written for scientists. We want everyone to engage with the book according to their interests. Any parts can be skipped. One part that may best help you understand how women respond to tickling are the descriptions they gave of their personal experiences. These descriptions are put in italics and a slightly smaller font. Quotes from different women are put in different paragraphs.

At the end of the book is a chapter titled *Take Away Messages* that summarizes in simple terms what we believe are the most important results from the study.

We think one reading of the book will be interesting for you. However, as with every book that has a lot of information, you will learn more from a second reading.

If you choose to read the tables, it will help to know the definitions of the following:

- **N** stands for number. It means the total number of participants in the corresponding row or column.
- Cumulative percentage is the percentage of of the women in that category plus the percentage in all lower categories. For example, we divide the women into five categories depending on the last time that they were tickled. The percentage of women who were tickled less than a week ago was 34%. The percentage tickled less recently than 1 week ago but more recently than 1 month ago was 31%. Therefore, the cumulative percentage tickled less than one month ago (those tickled less than a week ago plus between 1 week and 1 month ago) was 31% + 34% = 65%. Only a few tables discuss cumulative percentages, and they are not essential to understanding the results.

Some information was put in the Appendix to avoid burdening readers not interested in scientific details. These details include why only women were studied, what were their characteristics, what information they provided, and why the number of participants varied greatly from table to table and even within some tables. This information is not necessary to understand the results, but it may help you understand aspects of the study that seem strange.

We only reported results that were highly statistically significant using universally accepted statistical methods. However, results based on greater numbers of participants are more precise and likely to be more similar to results from future studies.

HOW INTERESTED ARE WOMEN IN TICKLING?

We begin the book by examining whether the study participants found tickling interesting. Almost half of the women, 45%, had a strong or very strong interest in tickling and 36% had searched for information about tickling on the internet at least once in the past year. These numbers are likely higher than in the general population because the women surveyed had volunteered to participate in a study about tickling.

Level of Interest in Tickling (N =1022)	
None	8%
Little	16%
Moderate	31%
Strong	28%
Very strong	17%

Number of Times Searched for Articles About Tickling in The Past Year (N=888)	
Never	64%
1 or 2	26%
3 to 5	5%
More than 5	4%

Two traits of the women particularly influenced their interest in tickling. One was whether or not they enjoyed being ticklish. Of 393 women who liked being ticklish, 64% had a strong interest in tickling, but only 33% of the 387 women who did not like being ticklish were interested. Another trait that strongly influenced a woman's interest in tickling was her ticklishness. Of 310 very ticklish women, 67% of had a strong interest in tickling compared to 29% of 269 women who were less than very ticklish.

Both the interest in tickling and the use of the internet to find out about tickling strongly differed by group. African and Muslim participants showed a greater interest in tickling than other groups (more than 50% had a strong interest) and Latin Americans had the least interest, only 28%. On the other hand, Asians were more likely to search the internet than other groups, 55%, and Latin Americans were least likely to search the internet, 19%. We do not know enough about these cultures to explain the results or even to be able to assess whether they accurately reflect the various cultures in the group. We have less confidence in the comparison of groups of countries than we do in any other results in this book.

Interest in Tickling by Group			
Group	N	% Strong interest	% Internet use
Africa	113	53%	43%
Asia	385	48%	55%
English culture	46	46%	33%
Europe	267	38%	31%
Latin America	97	28%	19%
Muslim	113	57%	44%
All women	1021	45%	42%

HOW FREQUENTLY ARE WOMEN TICKLED?

One thing that the study makes clear is that women are commonly tickled. About a third of the women surveyed had been tickled within the last week, and almost two thirds had been tickled within the last month.

Last Time Tickled (N=919)		
Category of last time tickled	% In category	*Cumulative %
Less than 1 week	34%	34%
1 week to 1 month	31%	65%
1 to 6 months	19%	84%
6 months to 2 years	9%	94%
More than 2 years	6%	100%
*Cumulative % means the sum of the percents in that row and all previous rows. For example, 34% of the women had not been tickled within the last week, and 65% had been tickled within the past month (34% and 31%).		

More ticklish women were tickled more frequently. The percentage of women tickled in the last week was lower for the women who reported that they were little or moderately ticklish, 27%, as compared to 45% of the women who were very or extremely ticklish.

VARIATION IN FREQUENCY BY GROUP

The variation across groups in the percentage of women who had been tickled in the last week was apparently by chance. It was amazing how similar the percentages of the women were. There was no outlier. This suggests that the frequency of tickling for women is only slightly influenced by culture.

The Percentage of Women in Each Group Who Had Been Tickled in the Last Week		
Group	N	% Tickled in last week
Africa	92	41%
Asia	367	31%
English culture	41	44%
Europe	234	32%
Latin America	91	35%
Muslim	94	43%
All women	919	34%

There was a suggestion in the data that older women were tickled less often, but there was an insufficient number of older women with this information to be certain. In any case, at least some of the older women who participated in this study were still being tickled. Of the 93 women over the age of 45, 25% had been tickled in the last week.

The Percentage of Participants in Each Age Range Who Were Tickled in the Last Week		
Age range	N	% Tickled in last week
18-25	262	39%
26-35	349	35%
36-45	215	32%
46-60	72	22%
Over 60	21	33%
All women	919	34%

VARIATION IN FREQUENCY BY RELATIONSHIP STATUS

The frequency with which the women were tickled depended on their romantic involvement. Women were least likely to be tickled within the last week if they were not in a romantic relationship (24%) and most likely to be tickled if they were dating (45%). This is convincing evidence that tickling is most common in romantic relationships, especially in the early stages.

The Percentage of Women in Each Type of Romantic Relationship Who Were Tickled in the Last Week		
	N	% Tickled in last week
Married	392	37%
Committed	177	31%
Dating	152	45%
Currently not in relationship	198	24%
All women	919	34%

Although many women were tickled by their friends or family, most tickling was done by their romantic partners for either sex or play.

Relationship of the Women to Their Most Frequent Ticklers (N=904)	
Spouse or partner	58%
Family member	26%
Friend	15%
Disliked person	1%

When we examined the percentage of women most often tickled by their romantic partner by region, we found it was greatest for Muslims. Muslim participants explained this finding to be the result of a strong prohibition in the Muslim culture against women being tickled by anyone other than their husbands. Since fewer people are allowed to tickle women in a Muslim culture, a higher percentage of the tickling is done by husbands or romantic partners. The Asian and Latin American women were less likely to be tickled by their romantic partners than other groups, but it was still about 50%.

The Percentage of Ticklish Women in Each Group Who Were Most Often Tickled by Their Romantic Partner		
	N	% Most often tickled by partner
Africa	91	69%
Asia	363	46%
English culture	41	66%
Europe	228	66%
Latin America	87	52%
Muslim	94	79%
All women	904	58%

CULTURAL BOUNDARIES FOR TICKLING

In all cultures, there were restrictions regarding who could be tickled. One person from Mexico observed that tickling in her culture usually showed sexual interest.

> *Mexico Culturally speaking, tickling is seen as more of a playful interaction between lovers than between friends or family members. I'm not sure if it is because society here gives it a sexual intention, but it is rare to see adults tickling adults or adults tickling older children. The only time parents tickle their kids is when they're younger than 5. I've noticed that small children will rarely tickle other small children. It is not widely seen.*

In contrast to the Mexican woman's report, a woman from India said that social tickling was common.

> *India When it comes to my culture, anything funny leading to a sarcastic or witty statement during a conversation normally leads to tickling.*

Of course, the above woman does not represent all of India. Rural areas were apparently more restrictive.

 After my marriage, my lifestyle had taken a poor transition, that I was married to a conventional family, who had restrictions regarding clothes and other basic cultures, even while it came to talking with others around the house. So, in my culture, post-marriage, in the new locality (a small town in the southern state of Kerala with mostly conventional people) *did restrict me from tickling others and also being tickled.*

<u>India</u> <u>UAE</u> *My culture is more modern than that of my friends whom I am currently with. My parents are quite open-minded when it comes to most things, and as is in the case of tickling too. I always had the freedom to get tickled and also tickle others,*

<u>India</u> *I was brought up in a mixed culture. Also, my dad being quite older than my mom. So, it was only my dad who restricted me from entering into tickling games and making a mess. Otherwise, the rest of my family could accept the fun and vibe of being tickled and tickling others.*

Several women said that Islam prohibits males from tickling females who are not their wives, sisters, or children.

<u>Morocco</u> *Islam says that tickling is normal and accepted, if a male was tickling you, it is only allowed if it was your brother, father or son, basically males who are blood related to you, other males can't touch you even if they were friends, while females can tickle each other even if it was a stranger.*

Even in liberal communities, it is not okay to tickle older people (with some exceptions for parents) or people of the opposite gender.

India Being from the Southern state of Tamil Nadu (with people who are comparatively better in culture and have their own spiritual beliefs) in India, in my culture, it is okay to tickle others who are younger than me. While tickling elders is not accepted and considered disrespectful. Also, when it comes to gender, there are restrictions as to where to touch and where not to. Therefore, tickling people of opposite genders whether elder or younger is not encouraged, especially while in a public place or gathering.

India I went to a city college finally to gain more exposure and my interest to learn and live a city life. That's when I saw all the rich and well-off kids, who most of the time had only fun. This sight was an entirely different one to me, where I came up from seeing only less wealthy and unhappy people. Hence, I did take time to adapt to acts like tickling in my college. And when I went home for vacations and tried these on my parents, they did not feel so happy about it and even questioned me if I was taught to do these at college and if I did these with boys.

If the line of appropriate behavior were crossed, the punishment could be severe.

India Talking about the worst experience, it was while I was only in the 8th Grade. It was my grandfather's death anniversary, and a lot of Pooja and rituals were happening. But being a kid, I was not so serious about the situation and was playful around. I went and kept on tickling my uncles, who were all so serious. The person who was carrying out the rituals signaled my aunt to put me into some other room, and she had to do it. Yes, she locked me up in a room for almost 2 hours, which I consider to be the worst 2 hours of my life, feeling all lonely and alone.

One attitude that was expressed by a Nigerian woman, but is probably found in other cultures, was the concern that tickling results in moral degradation.

<u>Nigeria</u> In addition, in Africa, physical touch was a big deal. Society believes that when a child, especially a female, is tickled, they are being trained to become promiscuous. There was a day a neighbor told us a story of a popular prostitute down our street. She explained that the prostitute used to be innocent like us until people started tickling her. She said what started as innocent as tickling led her into prostitution.

An African-American woman expressed similar values in her culture.

<u>U.S.</u> Tickling elders was often not well received, tickling in a public place between children was quickly put to rest, tickling people of opposite genders was mostly practiced between children or part-ners. Avoidance of intimate areas of the body when tickling was also practiced.

HOW TICKLISH ARE WOMEN?

The participants in this study ranged from not ticklish at all to feeling tickled just by thinking about it. The comments below suggest how much the ticklishness of the women varied.

Surprisingly, non-ticklish women could be just as annoyed by attempted tickling as ticklish women.

> *I was not ticklish as a child. A poke under the arm or a squeeze to the back of my neck or knee only annoyed or occasionally hurt me. It wasn't a question of whether or not I enjoyed being tickled. I just didn't have a tickle sensation for years.*

Other extremely ticklish participants reacted with uncontrolled laughter, screaming, coughing, or inability to breathe.

> *Without knowing the reaction, she tickled me around my hip region, where I would feel ticklish the most. I reacted so spontaneously that I almost fell from the chair and continued to laugh like an insane.*

> *Even after being 26. I still feel ticklish and that too to a level where if anyone just touches me to the vulnerable spot of my body, I start jumping and sometimes, no not sometimes but mostly shouting.*

Some women were very sensitive to tickling all over their bodies.

> *I am a very ticklish person. Every inch of my being, when touched, makes me wiggle and scream.*

> *I consider myself a person who is very ticklish, I feel it in my feet, knee, thigh, groin, between my legs (this is my most sensitive place to tickling) I also feel it in my belly, ribs, chest, neck, armpits and on the back of the neck. In short, I feel ticklish all over my body.*

In some cases, the tickling sensations came from more than just fingers.

> *Although there were times when people tried tickling me on my thighs, with their elbows (a very common tickling trick here), I never felt it so interesting as I was only less sensitive to it.*

One source of tickling was inanimate objects.

> *I have a very sensitive body, sometimes my clothes started ticking me when I sit in a bus with open windows.*

> *Spa is not for me. Remembering the massage slippers, that tickles too much. I don't know how old people can wear it and walk for long time. I can't last long wearing that.*

Several women responded to being tickled without being touched. The mere thought of being tickled was enough to trigger the same responses as a touch would.

I am ticklish almost everywhere on my body. I laugh whenever someone wiggles their fingers towards me or even suggests tickling.

I am ticklish to such an extent that I start laughing at the slightest touch. I laugh even when I am touched accidentally or even from the thought of being tickled.

In case you want me to jump from my seat and run through the whole house laughing like a psychopath all you have to do is show me your fingers and say the magic word 'tickle'. There you go! Your task is accomplished, my friend. I'm an extremely tickle-sensitive person. Believe me, while I'm writing it, I can feel the butterflies in my stomach, so you better know now how ticklish I am.

(report of a group discussion of women) From there we moved onto the question of how they felt when they knew that someone was about to tickle them. Most agreed that it is both exciting and scary at the same time. The feeling of anticipation alone can make you laugh just in knowing that it is going to happen. It can almost be as ticklish as the real thing even though no actual contact had yet taken place.

On the other hand, another woman said that anticipation could save her from being ticklish.

If we are all ready to get playful and stuff, yes we can feel ticklish during the time. But instead, it has also worked for me if I make a mindset to control getting tickled, then I tend to be less expressive and can behave as if I am not ticklish (although this is possible only about 60% of the time and dependent on the part of the body I am tried to be tickled).

Ticklishness can sometimes be a social disability. Some women reported problems they had from not being able to control their laughter.

One time my mother was scolding me for breaking a cup in the kitchen. I got a glimpse of my sister behind my mother, and she grinned and started making the tickling motions again. I found myself unable to control my laughter and cracked a smile. My mother noticed and got even madder at me to see me laughing.

I can recall several times when I would burst into repeated laughter when the pedicurist would touch my feet in the process of applying nail polish on my toes.

SELF-RATING OF TICKLISHNESS

The following table shows how ticklish the women were. Women rated their overall ticklishness on a scale from 1 (not at all ticklish) to 5 (extremely ticklish). Scores of 1 or 2 were considered not very ticklish, and scores of 4 or 5 were considered very ticklish. About half of the women were very ticklish, and only 19% were not at all or only slightly ticklish. The 19% may be low because, during the initial parts of the study, there were efforts to include only ticklish women.

Ticklishness of the Women (N =1600)	
Category	% In category
Not at all or some	20%
Moderately	26%
Very or extremely	54%

THE MOST TICKLISH AREAS

In general, there are a few go-to sites to give a good tickle: the bottoms of the feet, under the arms, and along the sides and ribs. These sites are commonly ticklish, but many other sites can be as well.

I am a very ticklish person. I get tickly everywhere, mostly on my belly and the soles of my feet.

I think my face and neck are the most sensitive to tickling. Next would be the armpits, arms, and legs.

I am more ticklish around the neck and also around my hip. Whenever anyone tickles me around my neck and hip area, I feel laughing to the extreme end. Though the feeling of ticklish triggers me for an extreme laughter yet it feels quite good to me. While tickling me I dislike the most, if anybody tickles me around my underarms. Apart from feeling ticklish I feel quite irritated and asks the person to remove his or her hand from the ticklish part of my body.

Personally, my underarms and my torso in general are not very ticklish. I am more ticklish on my erogenous areas. These include my neck, feet, knee area, and thighs. I am more sensitive in these areas.

When I am tickled on my neck, sometimes I am more annoyed, because I am very sensitive and protective of my neck. Even when people close to me tickle me on my neck, I sometimes feel a complex mix of laughter but also annoyance or even anger if I am focusing on something else or did not wish to be touched in that moment.

The next table shows where the women were ticklish according to their questionnaire responses. The sites that were most often very ticklish were, not surprisingly, the feet, sides, and underarms. The neck is also quite ticklish. This is used to support a theory about why people evolved to be ticklish. In this theory, ticklishness taught people to protect vulnerable sites in the body, and the neck is especially vulnerable. However, as the table also shows, the bottom of the feet and the thighs are also often quite ticklish. Because these sites are not more vulnerable than other less ticklish sites, their ticklishness cannot be used to support that theory.

Ticklishness by Site			
Location	N	Ticklishness	
		Not very	Very
Feet	1020	29%	45%
Sides or ribs	1020	31%	43%
Underarm	1281	32%	42%
Neck	1020	37%	39%
Belly	674	38%	37%
Thigh	1281	41%	36%
Breast	1020	44%	32%
Crotch	868	46%	32%
Navel	607	44%	29%
Ear or face	413	48%	29%
Behind knees	1020	48%	25%
Vulva	1281	52%	25%
Perineum	607	52%	25%
Back	1281	52%	23%
Butt	1020	62%	17%

PHYSICAL RESPONSES TO TICKLING

The participants were asked how often they laughed or wiggled when they were tickled. Possible answers to each question were on a 5-point scale from 1 (never laughing or wiggling) to 5 (always reacting in this way). For both laughing and wiggling, almost half of the women, 45%, marked "Always" while more than one-quarter marked "Never to sometimes". In most cases, the women gave a similar answer to how much they laughed or wiggled, but 9% of the time the answer varied by 2 or more points on a 5-point scale. These results show that laughing and wiggling are both reliable responses to being tickled. Presumably, evolution selected both the laughing and wiggling responses because they made women more attractive.

Frequency of Laughing and Wiggling (N= 305)		
Frequency	Laugh	Wiggle
Never to sometimes	28%	29%
Usually	28%	26%
Always	45%	45%

The most important trait that predicted whether women laughed or wiggled in response to being tickled was, not surprisingly, how ticklish they were. As shown in the table below, laughing and wiggling occurred for two-thirds of women who were extremely ticklish. For women whose ticklishness was moderate or less, only about one-quarter of the women, 24%, responded to tickling by always laughing or wiggling.

The Relationship Between Ticklishness and Physical Responses			
Ticklishness	N	Always laugh	Always wiggle
Average or less (1-3)	124	24%	24%
Very (4)	107	54%	53%
Extreme (5)	77	69%	68%
All women	308	45%	45%

REGIONAL DIFFERENCES

The responses to tickling could differ for women across regions because of variations in genes, culture, or how the study was managed. If there are no differences among the regions, then it is likely that the regions do not differ strongly in any way that could affect the response.

A table showing these differences is below. There were no statistical differences found across regions with respect to always laughing. If there is a difference among these regions, it is unlikely to be strong. This was surprising because some women in African and Asian countries expressed that it was not considered appropriate for them to laugh loudly when tickled. If we make the safe assumption that the cultures are quite different, then the similarity of results across cultures suggests that culture has little effect. Therefore, the differences among individuals are probably genetically-based.

Physical Responses to Tickling by Group		
	N	Always laugh	Always wiggle
Africa	27	37%	26%
Asia	111	49%	37%
English culture	6	NA	NA
Europe	95	42%	55%
Latin America	20	35%	55%
Muslim	45	51%	53%
All women	304	45%	45%

On the other hand, there was statistical evidence that Asians were less likely to always wiggle than women from other regions. Since there were no women who said it was inappropriate to wiggle when tickled, we don't know what to make of this finding.

ABILITY TO CONCEAL TICKLISHNESS

In general, ticklish women respond to tickling quickly. Nearly half of the participants responded within 5 seconds, and only 6% said they could last longer than 30 seconds.

Number of Seconds Can Pretend to Not Be Ticklish				
N	5 or less	6 to 15	15 to 30	More than 30
921	46%	38%	11%	6%

A few women described a total inability to avoid responding to tickles. Whether they wanted to or not, being tickled would force them into fits of laughter and squirming.

> *I can't make myself not ticklish. I can't control laugh when someone do tickling to me.*

You asked about being able to hold still when tickled, without laughing or squirming. Well, for me, it's not possible, though at first, I try not to laugh or react, then I just can't help it, I get to react.

However, only 15% of the women said that they were ticklish in all circumstances. Many said that they were not ticklish under some circumstances, such as when they were in a bad mood or when it was socially unacceptable for them to respond to tickling.

Circumstances Not Ticklish (N=308)	
Always Ticklish	15%
Bad mood	53%
Wrong person tickling	46%
In public	42%
Medical examination	34%

For women who can control their ticklishness, however, there are good reasons for doing so:

1. Having a known sensitivity to tickling made them a target.
2. Responding to tickling encourages the tickler and makes them believe they welcomed the tickling.
3. Laughing, especially in response to tickles, is not socially acceptable in the current setting.

In front of my boyfriend's parents I tried not to laugh too loudly. I tried to appear serious, responsible, and intelligent before allowing them to see my playful and silly sides.

Some women can control their physical responses to tickling, even though the tickling makes them want to laugh and squirm.

> *I am ticklish but also have developed a skill to act as if I'm not ticklish at times. I also enjoy being tickled and am happy about it. I love to laugh out loud when being tickled provided it is okay in a particular situation and by familiar people.*

> *I'm ticklish but I can hold myself from laughing, squirming, or wiggling. I'm glad I'm ticklish and glad I can hold myself and pretend not to be ticklish.*

> *I can hold myself not to laugh especially when I'm angry or being tickled by someone I'm not close to.*

> *I have had to learn how not to laugh out loud immediately when tickled. I am however, in most cases, unable to control my facial expression in response to things like tickling. I have also been known to show my emotions on my face most of the time. I have also trained myself to keep my body still in most situations when I am being tickled for the safety of my partner.*

For some women, ticklishness is a choice that can be turned off either partly or completely, at least in some situations.

> *I can switch off if I give myself time to do it but, if I am caught unawares, I cannot, because I would need to mentally prepare myself first.*

Whether these people switched off their ticklishness often depended on the consequences of responding to the tickles.

I was highly influenced by the people around me while being tickled. As I even had to control my reactions depending on people around me, like that in the case of my stepdad. If it's my stepdad, I have very little relationship with him and hence express pretty little in any sort of situation. Like even if someone tickles me in front of him, I just don't react much, as I feel that gap.

It is normal to resist being tickled by keeping yourself from being ticklish, and I am no exception. I have kept myself from being ticklish in numerous incidents due to various reasons. For instance, I have kept myself from being ticklish when interacting with sexually attracted men, and I don't feel the same. Letting someone who wants to have sex with you tickle you will obviously send a seductive message to them that you are into them, which in most cases is not always the case.

METHODS TO CONCEAL

Strategies used by the women to avoid being ticklish include focusing on breathing, stiffening the tickled area, and using brute mental control.

I mostly tune my reactions on being tickled based on my feelings during the particular situation. I have developed a capability, a sort of control to not feel ticklish, not just me, I have seen my cousins also have the same trick. It's just mere control, where I sort of prepare myself to be less sensitive to tickling by just stiffening my body part wherever I think one is gonna tickle me, especially in places like the neck and legs.

If I don't feel like being tickled, I will control my mind not to feel and show any reaction.

Since being a child and hating the way my sister taunted me, I gained the ability to turn off my ticklishness. This meant that as a teenager and young adult, I was able to discourage classmates, friends and dates from tickling me by focusing on my breathing and not reacting. People would try to tickle me under my arms or on my toes but I was able to control it and refused to let them make me laugh.

If I concentrate really hard and let my mind drift away from the tickling, it can be suppressed for some time.

One specific situation in which several women reported not being ticklish was during sex, when stronger sensations distracted them from the sensation of tickling.

(A discussion of a group of women) They felt that if you were deeper into the moment, their ticklish sensitivity would disappear as none of the group reported having to laugh in the middle of having sex. But, in the early stages, they could still be sensitive to being tickled.

WHAT INFLUENCES TICKLISHNESS?

To understand ticklishness, it's necessary to understand what influences it. In this study, we evaluated what is related to ticklishness. Being related is not the same as influencing, but sometimes it gives a clue about influences.

TICKLISHNESS OF THE MOTHER

Ticklishness depends on our genes— probably almost entirely on our genes. So why even bother to test whether ticklish mothers have ticklish daughters? One reason is that sometimes what we think we'll find isn't exactly what we do find. A second reason is that confirmatory findings help show the validity of the data. A third is that publishing only surprising findings gives them too much credibility. A fourth reason is that there may be something in the details of the results that narrows possible explanations.

An interesting, if not surprising result, was that the more ticklish a woman was, the more likely she was to have a very ticklish daughter. This is consistent with there being many genes for ticklishness, and the more of these genes the mother had, the more likely her daughter would be very ticklish.

Unfortunately, our beautiful results had a stain; mothers who were not ticklish at all had a high percentage of daughters who were very ticklish. The only explanation we could come up with was that many participants who said that their mothers were not ticklish at all really didn't know if that was true because they had never discussed it or tried to tickle them. In a future test of the mother/daughter relationship, we could exclude data from mothers if their daughters did not know how ticklish they were.

The Percentage of Very Ticklish Women According to the Ticklish Score of Their Mothers		
Ticklish score of mothers	N	% Of daughters who were very ticklish
1 (Not at all)	135	42%
2	207	25%
3	315	33%
4	195	51%
5 (Extremely)	138	62%
All women	579	40%

VARIATION IN TICKLISHNESS BY AGE

Age has to be related to ticklishness because age is related to everything. Nerve sensitivity decreases with age, which might decrease ticklishness. On the other hand, the tolerance of strong sensations may also decrease with age, which might make tickling more annoying. According to the women's reports, there were no obvious trends. About one third of the women reported no changes in ticklishness with age and similar percentages reported an increase or decrease in ticklishness.

Reported Change in Ticklishness After Childhood (N = 1024)	
Greater	37%
Unchanged	31%
Less	32%

More Ticklish with Age

The following comments are from women who became more ticklish with age.

I feel like mine has increased over the years. I have become even more sensitive towards it and very reactive, and now, when someone even tries to come at me with the intention, my expressions say it all.

One woman explained that her greater ticklishness came about through greater psychological maturity.

I'm not sure when the change occurred, but one day—as an adult—I experienced tickling sensations. Curiously, my tickle sensations have increased with age. This may give some credence to the theories that indicate ticklishness is tied to social conditioning. Perhaps changes in my body, comfort and stability in my relationships, and increased self-confidence have allowed me to be more open to tickling sensations. Perhaps my education and life experiences have offered me better recognition of scenes where tickling can be safe and pleasurable. I have learned to protect myself against scenarios where tickling can be harmful and dangerous. I have to admit — deep down, I feel grateful that I finally have some level of ticklishness. The child in me still wants to experience the joy that

*I see others express. And the adult in me finds it comforting that I
am in relationships where I can enjoy the physical and emotional
pleasure of loving and safe tickles.*

A common explanation for becoming more ticklish with age
was a greater awareness or acceptance of new sensations.

*I'm not sure why I became more ticklish, maybe I just became
more aware of it.*

*Think of it like it's puberty or just growing up and becoming more
sensitive, more parts of my body opening up to new feelings I had
no idea were there. Let's say I got more sensitive to tickles, and
touches in general which explains why I am more ticklish now as
an adult than as a child.*

One source of greater awareness was tickling by boyfriends.

*As a child I was one child of parents therefore no one usually tickle
me but after 18 my boyfriend start tickle me and I realized I am
more ticklish than before. In the age of 18, I use to know that I feel
tickle on under arms and sides just but now i feel ticklish on thighs,
vulva, clit, naval etc.*

Another woman realized that her ticklishness grew along with
her sexual feelings.

*I can say that I have been more ticklish now than when I was 18. I
have noticed it since I started going out with my first date. I believe
there are some kind of feelings that when we are touched or tickled*

by the one that we intimately want, our body quickly responds to it in a form of arousal and that's how I perceived tickling now that I am an adult.

Less Ticklish with Age

While many women believed they became more ticklish with age, others reported being less ticklish than when they were younger. There are several plausible explanations for this.

One is that ticklishness does not change as much as how ticklish the women act.

I feel like girls at school used to act more ticklish and you know just laugh out loud and make a lot of noise for the fun and sake of grabbing attention, but while we grow older, we tend to be more aware and alert and only react based on the situation/comfort zone.

A second explanation is that the change in sensitivity was due to the effects of aging.

As I age, my most sensitive body parts become less active as my giggle response goes down for various reasons, including hormonal changes and other adulthood stressful situations. Like any other normal person, aging has interfered with my nerves and receptors, making my body less sensitive to tickling.

Another woman became less ticklish with age, but her decrease in ticklishness was related to psychological changes rather than age.

I would have said that my ticklish score was a 5 when I was in school, but in my adulthood, I have found that there are some instances when I am not very ticklish. Another aspect of this I have considered is that I have generalized anxiety, depression, and ADHD. Part of these conditions is either less sensitivity at times, in the case of depression, or more sensitivity at times, in the case of anxiety and ADHD. In the past, I was most often anxious and restless, so I feel that my sensitivity was heightened at that time. After having experienced more hardship in recent years, I have found that my response to tickling varies more.

It is also possible that women only thought they were less ticklish because they learned how to avoid being tickled and became less aware of how ticklish they were. However, none of the women in this study gave that explanation.

One woman suggested that it was because her interpretation of tickles changed with age.

I would be right to say I'm less ticklish than I was back then. Again, I think it may just depend on my closeness to that person. Some persons just touch my knee or leg and I get really irritated by that simple action.

In some cases, the women learned how to make themselves less ticklish.

I would say I'm less ticklish now. When I was very young, I used to laugh when being tickled until I cried. But it's a different case now as a young adult, I don't give in to it even when it comes as

*a surprise from a friend. If I can keep myself from laughing and
squirming even when I'm anticipating being tickled or when it
comes as a surprise, I think I'm less ticklish.*

After a certain age, physiological changes rather than will or
attitude may have the greatest effect on ticklishness. Our data,
however, gave no conclusive evidence showing that ticklishness
decreased with age, although there was a suggestion that it was
lower in women over the age of 60.

The Percentage of Participants in Each Age Range Who Were Very Ticklish		
Age range	N	% very ticklish
18-25	564	56%
26-35	643	55%
36-45	179	50%
46-60	119	47%
Over 60	34	32%
All women	1539	54%

Comparing the ticklishness of women in different age groups is
not the best way to measure changes in ticklishness over time.
It's much better to evaluate the ticklishness of the same woman
over 40 years. We look forward to checking back in 40 years to
see how the results from the big boys' study compares to ours.

VARIATION IN TICKLISHNESS AROUND THE WORLD

Variation in ticklishness by geographic region could be caused
by differences in genetics or culture. We compared the percentage of participants who were very ticklish for the six groups
surveyed. The rates ranged from a low of 43% for women who

came from countries with an English culture to a high of 59%
for women from Asia. The difference among these rates did not
occur by chance, but we do not know whether the differences
were due to regional variations in genes, cultures, the characteristics of the volunteers, or reporting a given degree of ticklishness. There was evidence that the women from the Asian and
Muslim countries were most ticklish. This would make sense if
Asians were more prone to be ticklish because a high percentage
of the Muslims were from Pakistan and Bangladesh.

Whatever the limitations of the data are, it is almost certain
that a high percentage of women throughout the world are
very ticklish.

The Percentage of Women in Each Group Who Were Very Ticklish		
Group	N	% Very ticklish
Africa	201	49%
Asia	698	59%
English culture	93	43%
Europe	241	49%
Latin America	187	47%
Muslim	180	58%
All women	1600	54%

VARIATION IN TICKLISHNESS BY RELATIONSHIP STATUS

It is not obvious how being frequently tickled affects ticklishness.
Do bodies frequently tickled become less ticklish because they
learn how to ignore or resist the sensation of tickling, or do
bodies rarely tickled lose their ticklishness without constant
reminders or sensitization?

One obvious test of the effect of tickling on ticklishness is a comparison of frequently and infrequently tickled women. It turns out that 69% of the participants who were tickled in the last week were very ticklish compared to only 41% of the women who had not been tickled for more than six months. That should settle it—the more a woman is tickled, the more ticklish she is.

The Percent of Participants Who Were Very Ticklish According to the Last Time They Were Tickled		
Last Time Tickled	N	% Very ticklish
Less than 1 week	180	69%
One week to six months	227	56%
More than six months	69	41%
All Women	476	59%

The only flaw with this explanation is that it puts the cart before the horse. Instead of tickling increasing ticklishness, ticklishness increases tickling, i.e., the more ticklish a woman is, the more others want to tickle her. It's more fun that way.

Another way of testing whether the frequency of tickling was related to ticklishness was to compare the ticklishness of women according to their type of relationship. As reported earlier in the book, 45% of participants who were currently dating had been tickled in the last week. However, only 24% of the participants who were not in a relationship had been tickled in the past week. If ticklishness were influenced by the frequency of being tickled, we would expect to find a large difference in ticklishness between dating women and those not in a relationship. What we found was nada (which means "nothing" for those of you behind in your Spanish lessons). As shown in the table below,

54% of the women studied were very ticklish, and there was no evidence that it varied by relationship. Our conclusion is that the frequency of being tickled has little, if any, effect on ticklishness.

Percentage of Participants Who Are Very Ticklish According to Relationship Status			
Relationship status	% Tickled inlast week (from other data)	N	% Very ticklish
1 No current	24%	417	50%
2 Dating	45%	245	55%
3 Committed	31%	260	55%
4 Married	37%	647	56%
All women	34%	1581	54%

PERSONALITY TRAITS THAT PREDICT TICKLISHNESS

Our original intent was to examine the role of tickling around the world. As the study progressed, we began to add questions that would help us look for clues about what influences either the sensation of tickling or how our brain interprets that sensation. Because many participants thought that personality traits could be predictive, additional questions were added about personality. This makes sense because, like ticklishness and response to tickling , personality traits also depend on underlying physiological and neurological characteristics that influence how people react. Of course, finding a relationship between traits does not explain either trait. However, if relationships are found, they might guide future research about the reasons for the relationships.

For this study, we collected information on 25 personality traits. Some of them were suggested by the participants, while others were commonly used in research studies. The number of participants who provided information on a given trait varied from 807 to 139 depending on which questionnaires asked about the trait. We are most confident in the evaluation of traits assessed by questions given to larger groups of participants.

Statistical methods were used to determine which traits were related to ticklishness. All of the related traits were then ranked by how strongly they were correlated with ticklishness; the trait with the rank of 1 has the highest correlation with ticklishness. To simplify the discussion, the traits were categorized into groups, as shown below. The number before each trait is the rank for the correlation. If there is no rank, then the correlation might have been caused by chance alone.

Ranks of Personality Traits [a,b] for Their Relationship to Ticklishness	
Name of group of traits	**Traits within the group**
Attitude to physical contact	**4 enjoy sex**, 11 like caresses, like hugs,
Sociability	2 try to please, 4 likable
Assertiveness	6 like winning, 9 confident, dislike criticism
Acceptance of risk	1 like security, **7 like risk**
Psychological health	**10 happy**
Intellectual	12 analytical, dislike routines, organized
Physiology	**3 nervous**, 8 dislike loud sounds, 10 dislike scratchy clothing, energetic

[a] There was convincing evidence that all traits in this table were related to ticklishness or attitude toward being tickled. Traits with no number predicted liking tickling, but they did not predict ticklishness. Other traits were studied that are not included in this table because they did not predict either ticklishness or enjoyment of tickling.

[b] The number before the trait is the rank of the correlations of that trait with ticklishness. **Bolded** names are used for traits with the strongest evidence for being an important predictor of ticklishness. For these traits, there was an increase in ticklishness for each increase in the trait. For example, the more women enjoyed sex the more ticklish they tended to be.

You will see from the tables below that none of these traits did a great job predicting ticklishness. In other words, some participants with a high level of the trait were not very ticklish, and some participants with a low level of the trait were very ticklish. We were not surprised by our inability to find personality traits that perfectly predict ticklishness because no personality trait is closely tied to a physical trait, but finding a relationship might increase understanding of what's involved with ticklishness.

Some personality traits that we expected to be associated with ticklishness were not, but they may be in another study that used different definitions or had more accurate information.

ATTITUDE TO PHYSICAL CONTACT

All traits in the group of attitudes toward physical contact were strongly related to ticklishness. Unexpectedly and fascinatingly, the trait most associated with being very ticklish (a rating of 4, or 5 on the 5-point ticklish scale), was liking sex. As shown in the table below, only 34% of the women who didn't enjoy sex very much (rating of 1 to 3) were very ticklish, compared to almost twice that percentage, 66%, who enjoy sex extremely (rating of 5). There might be a certain type of sensitivity that increases both ticklishness and sexual pleasure.

Support for this finding came from one participant who said,

When I am feeling most sensitive to physical touch in general is also when I enjoy sex the most.

The Percentage of Women Who Are Very Ticklish According to Their Rating for How Much They Enjoy Sex		
Enjoy sex	N	Very ticklish
Not a lot (1 or 2)	54	26%
Moderate (3)	113	35%
Very much (4)	185	57%
Extremely (5)	211	68%
All women	563	54%

Sensitivity to caresses is less intense than sexual sensitivity. Women with this type of sensitivity were also more ticklish; the percentage of very ticklish women increased from 35% for those who didn't much enjoy their lover's caresses to 61% for those who enjoyed them greatly. However, enjoyment of caresses had a weaker relationship with tickling than sexual pleasure did. Also, information about liking caresses was unrelated to ticklishness after using statistical methods that took into account, how much the women liked sex. Our conclusion was that the association between liking sex and ticklishness was something special that was not general to all sensations.

The Percentage of Women Who Are Very Ticklish According to Their Rating of Enjoyment Lover's Caresses		
Enjoy sex	N	Very ticklish
Low (1 to 3)	295	38%
High (4)	211	54%
Very high (5)	320	62%
All women	805	51%

SOCIABILITY

All four traits related to sociability were also related to ticklishness. Of these four traits, likability was the best predictor of ticklishness. However, since this estimate of the relationship was only based on information from 139 participants, the estimate is less precise than estimates based on more participants. In a different set of 139 participants, the relationship with likability will probably still exist, but it may be weaker than we found here.

The Relationship of the Percentage of Women Who Are Very Ticklish According to Their Rating for How Likeable They Are		
Likable	N	Very ticklish
Low (1 to 3)	50	24%
High (4 to 7)	89	55%
All women	139	44%

A possible reason that very likable people are more ticklish is that they want to be liked; therefore, they allow themselves to be ticklish even if it is uncomfortable.

The Relationship of the Percentage of Women Who Were Very Ticklish According to Their Desire to Please		
Desire to please	N	Very ticklish
Not Extreme (1 to 5)	103	36%
Extreme (7)	33	70%
All women	136	44%

Assertiveness

The results for liking winning are shown below. The women who most liked winning were almost four times as likely to be very ticklish as the least competitive women. All three measures of assertiveness had about the same relationship with being very ticklish.

The Percentage of Women Who Are Very Ticklish According to How Much They Like Winning		
Like winning	N	Very ticklish
Little (1 to 2)	26	15%
Moderate (3 to 5)	79	46%
Extreme (7)	34	62%
All women	139	44%

This relationship is real. We expected that the more assertive women would be less ticklish because they would fight loss of control. However, that was not the case; women who strongly liked winning, disliked criticism, and feared being controlled were often more ticklish.

ACCEPTANCE OF RISK

The strongest predictor of ticklishness was liking security. Of the 49 women with the greatest need for security, 60% were very ticklish compared to only 34% of the 90 women less interested in security. There was evidence that liking security was related to ticklishness, but the sample size was small, and the real relationship is unlikely to be as strong as what was observed in our sample.

The Percentage of Women Who Were Very Ticklish According to How Much They Liked Security		
Liked security	N	Very ticklish
Not extreme (1 to 5)	90	34%
Extremely (7)	49	60%
All women	139	44%

We also found that women who liked greater risk were more likely to be ticklish. Since it seems that women who liked greater risk would need less security, this result seems to directly contradict the one above. In case you wonder how anyone could be so stupid as to air their dirty laundry in public (show conflicting results), we have two answers. One is that we don't want to over-promote work that is the best we could do but, without question, flawed. A second is that, according to statistics, this result was not accidental. Maybe in the future, some tickling research fanatic will come up with an explanation that resolves the apparent contradiction. To the extent that there is a contradiction, however, our vote is for the results related to risk; the sample size is much larger and the increase in effect is shown in three groups, not just two.

The Percentage of the Women Who Were Very Ticklish According to How Much They Liked Taking Risks		
Like risk	N	Very ticklish
Low (1 to 4)	187	40%
Above Average (5 to 6)	159	57%
Extreme (7)	65	77%
All women	411	52%

PSYCHOLOGICAL HEALTH

A particularly interesting relationship was between ticklishness and happiness. Happiness was included in the questionnaires early in the study because several participants had the impression that happy people were ticklish. Because of the large number of women who answered the question about happiness, the estimated percentages were precise. Every increase in happiness was associated with an increase in the percentage of highly ticklish women.

One possible explanation is that happy people are happy about everything and don't try to suppress their ticklishness. Another is that the type of physiology that makes people happy also makes them ticklish. We have no evidence that either of these explanations is correct, but the results were strong enough that we expect this relationship to be found in other studies.

The Percentage of Women Who Are Very Ticklish According to Their Rating for Happiness		
Happiness	N	Very ticklish
Low (1 to 2)	46	32%
Average (3)	125	44%
Above average (4)	218	54%
High (5)	187	64%
All women	576	53%

PHYSIOLOGY

Another relationship that we expect to be verified in subsequent studies is the relationship between nervousness and ticklishness. Like the question about happiness, the question about nervousness was also included at the suggestion of participants. Only 25% of the least nervous participants were very ticklish compared to 70% of the most nervous participants. The evidence for an association with ticklishness is stronger for nervousness than for any other trait.

The Percentage of Women Who Are Very Ticklish According to Their Rating for Nervousness		
Nervousness	N	Very ticklish
Very low (1)	40	25%
Low (2 to 3)	95	35%
Moderate (4 to 5)	71	51%
High (6 to 7)	50	70%
All women	256	45%

Two plausible explanations for all the associations we found between personality traits and ticklishness were:

1. Some personality traits make women more sensitive or less resistant to tickling. This fits with a comment made by one of the women who contributed narrative information that she was more ticklish when she was anxious.
2. Some personality traits are caused by the same brain wiring that influences ticklishness.

We could not evaluate either of these hypotheses in this study.

A relationship that we expected but did not find was between pain tolerance and ticklishness. We had assumed that the tolerance of pain was either related to the sensitivity of the nerve fibers or the ability to suppress this sensitivity. We also assumed that the degree of ticklishness would be affected in the same way. However, we found no evidence that ticklishness was related to pain tolerance.

ENJOYMENT OF TICKLING

This chapter presents data on whether the women liked being tickled. Subsequent chapters will report on factors that influence liking to be tickled.

Liking to be tickled varies enormously, even among friends in the same culture. An example includes two women who were recruited by the same person in a discussion group. They are both very ticklish but experienced opposite reactions.

> *Just the thought of it make me feel ticklish all over my body...I don't enjoy it. It makes me feel suffocated.*

> *I start laughing, can't you see I have already started with its discussion only...A lot. I enjoy tickling.*

One way to find the percentage of women who like being tickled is to ask them. Their responses showed that this is a perfect question to prove that women are not all the same; 32% had at least a somewhat negative view (hated it, very negative, or slightly negative), 43% had a positive view (slightly positive, very glad or extremely glad), and 25% had a neutral view.

<table>
<tr><td colspan="3">Attitude Toward Being Ticklish
(N=725)</td></tr>
<tr><td>Attitude</td><td>% Per category</td><td>*Cumulative %</td></tr>
<tr><td>1 Hate it</td><td>7%</td><td>7%</td></tr>
<tr><td>2 Very negative</td><td>8%</td><td>15%</td></tr>
<tr><td>3 Slightly negative</td><td>17%</td><td>32%</td></tr>
<tr><td>4 Neutral</td><td>25%</td><td>57%</td></tr>
<tr><td>5 Slightly positive</td><td>21%</td><td>78%</td></tr>
<tr><td>6 Very glad</td><td>13%</td><td>90%</td></tr>
<tr><td>7 Extremely glad</td><td>10%</td><td>100%</td></tr>
<tr><td colspan="3">*Cumulative % is the % of all participants in that category or any previous categories.</td></tr>
</table>

We also asked whether they liked being tickled by their lover frequently or most of the time, and how much they enjoyed being tickled by their lover. We combined the results from the three questions to give us a single yes/no rating about being glad to be ticklish for 1548 participants.

All women who said they were glad to be ticklish were rated a yes and all women with a negative attitude were rated no. If the participant did not answer this question or she was neutral about being ticklish, we used the questions about how much she liked her lover tickling her or the question about whether she frequently liked her lover tickling her. If the answer to these questions was positive, then we rate the woman as liking being ticklish.

AREAS PREFERRED FOR TICKLES

Based on reports from 27 women about their preferred spots to be tickled, it is clear that the women differed.

My favorite places are the neck, sides, and inner thighs. My least favorite places are the belly and underarms

I am most ticklish under the legs, and it's also the least favorite place I like tickling. I love being tickled on the sides;

(From group discussion) She likes to be tickled, on her back, on her neck, and on her belly. She doesn't like the ones that are usually done under her armpits or on the sides of her back.

I am most comfortable with him tickling my back but I also enjoy the playful under the arm tickling from time to time.

I don't feel any excitement when tickled on my torso, but my neck, palms, area around my knees (my thighs in general), and feet are extremely ticklish. These are also my erogenous zones.

Under my feet, my lower back, my nipples, and my sides. Least favorite place is my upper back and thighs.

I like being tickled on my sides, under my feet and my upper back. I don't like being tickled in my armpits at all.

My favorite places are my nipples, my abdomen, my ears, my feet. My least favorite places are my legs, hand, thighs etc.

In a light mood, my favorite place to be tickled is my ribs. My least favorite places is my palms.

My most favorite place is my neck which is like the highest of all, then my armpit and even in between my ass line, Basically the upper part of my body has the most ticklish parts. My least favorite places to be tickled is my leg and hand.

The preferences for all 27 women were organized into a table. Of all the spots named, the favorite was being tickled on the neck; nine participants liked being tickled there and none disliked it. The back was another preferred area to be tickled; eight women liked being tickled there and only one disliked it. The most disliked areas to be tickled, on the other hand, were the thighs, underarms, and stomach.

Responses to Tickling From Answers to Essay Questions (N=27)		
Places	Liked	Disliked
Necks	9	
Sides	8	3
Back	8	1
Feet	7	4
Nipples	5	
Vulva	4	
Underarms	4	6
Stomach	4	4
Ears	3	
Knees	2	1
Waist	1	
Thighs	1	4
Hands	1	3
Breast	1	
Torso	1	

Preferences were not only for the area tickled but how the tickling was done.

> *Tickling consists of both the common with hands and also another one when the partner tickles with his beard/hair on the body. The 2nd one which I was talking about is a very tempting and more of sexual pleasure of tickling variant.*

HOW DEMOGRAPHIC FACTORS INFLUENCED LIKING TICKLING

In this chapter, we will examine whether liking tickling is affected by region, relationship status, age, or sexual preference.

There was strong evidence that enjoyment of being ticklish varied according to region. Africans were the most positive about ticklish and Latin Americans the least positive. These two outliers could have been caused by cultural differences, but it's also possible that the differences were caused by the culture of the women who did the recruiting. The evidence is strong that about 45% of the women in most regions have positive feelings about being tickled.

The Percentage Who Liked Being Ticklish by Group		
Group	N	Liked being ticklish
Africa	174	65%
Asia	655	45%
English culture	90	52%
Europe	224	40%
Latin America	243	31%
Muslim	163	45%
All women	1548	45%

Women who were not in a relationship had a less positive view toward tickling than others. Only 33% of the women not in a relationship liked being ticklish compared to more than 47% of the women who were in a relationship.

The Percentage Who Liked Being Ticklish According to Relationship Status		
Current relationship	N	Liked
Committed	243	47%
Dating	249	51%
Married	598	49%
None	429	33%
All women	1519	44%

Sexual preference was not found to be related to whether women were glad to be ticklish.

The Percentage Who Liked Being Ticklish According to Sexual Preference		
Sexual preference	N	Liked being ticklish
Men and women	52	48%
Men only	612	43%
Women only	29	48%
Never sexual relationship	26	35%
All women	721	43%

ANECDOTES ABOUT CHANGES WITH AGE

Many women said that their tolerance for tickling changed with age. Some became less tolerant, some more tolerant, and many became pickier about who had tickling rights.

Liked Less with Age

Some women who reported that they liked tickling less when they were older gave a psychological explanation.

> *When I was younger and those times before my marriage, I used to be comfortable wherever I was being tickled...I used to enjoy it. But as I grew older, I am not very comfortable when people tickle me. I just feel awkward and too old for it. I developed a feeling like why is this person tickling me...just because I am old.*

> *When we first started dating, tickling is one of our way to cuddle each other. We are both fond of this bonding since there's a lot of laughter, giggles and it's really fun. There are days when we're in some petty fights, one tickle from each other makes everything less serious. Sometimes, we used to tickle each other just to ease some tension between us. However, as time goes by, tickling is gradually fading, and it becomes something I personally hate. I became very sensitive as our relationship grows, and it makes me feel like tickling doesn't make sense.*

> *As a child, I always enjoyed being tickled — it was fun to laugh and playfully fight off my siblings or caretakers. However, as I've grown older, I've gained an unfavorable perspective that can only be blamed on my ever-growing anxiety, and dislike for the feeling of being helpless.*

One participant said that tickling became uncomfortable when she developed a physical ailment.

As a child I was like anyone else, very ticklish, wrestling around to protect my tickle spots. As a preteen, I discovered that my tickle spots were no longer ticklish at all, many tried anyway, but things were changing inside of me, my sense of feel was being changed due to fibromyalgia (a condition of the nerve endings) what once tickled, now caused me pain and bruising.

Some women were not less tolerant of tickling but instead became more selective in who could do the tickling.

Whenever someone tickles me, I can't withstand it long enough as I did when I was younger. On the other hand, I have become more ticklish with my romantic partner, in that I consider tickling more in terms of sexual arousal and not just for laughter and bonding. Since I became 18, I enjoy and appreciate being tickled by my partner and not any other person.

I think my attitudes have changed due to the way I view proximity, body familiarity and relationships in general. I have become selective to the people I play around with; I tend to be more aware of my body hence more sensitive when someone gets too close so that tickles becomes some sort of invasion when done by anyone I would not have accepted within my circle. I also do not like attention that much, thus I view tickles as some form of too much attention which I would rather forego except in special circumstances and for special people. Back in the day, it was just a fun and interactive activity.

Liked More with Age

Some women who became more tolerant of tickling when they were older attributed their greater tolerance to a greater self-awareness.

> *I think that generally people become more tolerant because they are older, and they are familiar with tickling.*

> *I became more self-aware and controlled, I guess.*

Less frequent tickling with age was not always the woman's choice. Some women who were tickled less missed being tickled.

> *As I grew up, it reduced because I felt more in control of my emotions, and there are not so many people who would want to tickle you. I also get to miss it so much, especially when we have arguments with my boyfriend, and he avoids me for a while. So, tickling after 18 wasn't as exciting as it was when I was a kid, but it arouses me when I am tickled in the right places.*

> *As an adult I do not have as much experience with tickling as I did when I was a child. Most people do not tickle me anymore. Perhaps that is a pity. I would like to have that same cheering feeling that I got from my mom tickling my feet.*

STATISTICAL ANALYSIS OF CHANGES WITH AGE

We expected that older age would reduce the tolerance of tickling. Liking tickling was lower in those older than age 45 (47% for women ages 26 to 45, but only 37% for participants ages 45 to

60 and 27% for those older than 60). However, it was also lower for participants ages 18 to 25, 41%. This may be because fewer of these women were in a romantic relationship, and views toward tickling were more positive for women in a romantic relationship.

The Percentage Who Liked Tickling According to Age		
Age range	N	Liked
18-25	554	41%
26-35	558	48%
36-45	225	46%
45-60	114	37%
Older than 60	37	27%
All women	1488	44%

Two-thirds of the participants said they had changed their attitude toward tickling since they were children. For the participants in this study, there was a slightly greater likelihood that their tolerance toward being tickled would increase rather than decrease (38% versus 30%).

Change in Tolerance of Tickling from Childhood to Adult (N =852)	
Tolerance	% In category
More tolerant	38%
Unchanged	32%
Less tolerant	30%

PERSONALITY TRAITS THAT PREDICT ENJOYMENT OF TICKLING

The same personality traits tested for predicting ticklishness were also tested for predicting enjoyment of tickling. There was strong evidence that 16 of the traits tested predicted the enjoyment of tickling. We ranked these traits from 1 to 16 based on how well they predicted the enjoyment of being tickled. Traits with almost the same ability to predict enjoyment of tickling were given the same ranking. Thus, seven of the traits that were almost tied for the third highest ranking were given the rank of 3. Because seven traits were given a rank of 3, the trait with the next highest ranking was given a rank of 10. Unless there was strong statistical evidence that the trait was related to the enjoyment of tickling, we did not give it a ranking.

<table>
<tr><td colspan="2" align="center">Traits Predicting [a,b] Enjoyment of Tickling</td></tr>
<tr><td>Name of group of traits</td><td>Traits within the group</td></tr>
<tr><td>Attitude to Physical Contact:</td><td>3 like hugs, 3 like caresses, 3 enjoy sex</td></tr>
<tr><td>Sociability</td><td>1 likable, 12 try to please</td></tr>
<tr><td>Assertiveness</td><td>3 like winning, 3 confident, 16 dislike criticism</td></tr>
<tr><td>Acceptance of Risk</td><td>3 like risk, like security</td></tr>
<tr><td>Psychological Health</td><td>15 happy</td></tr>
<tr><td>Intellectual:</td><td>2 analytical thinking, 13 dislike routines, 14 organized</td></tr>
<tr><td>Physiology:</td><td>3. energetic, 10 ticklish score, 11 nervous, dislike scratchy clothing, dislike loud sound</td></tr>
</table>

a There was convincing evidence that all traits in this table were related to ticklishness or attitude toward being tickled. Traits with no number predicted ticklishness, but it did not predict liking tickles. Other traits were studied that are not included in this table because they did not predict either ticklishness or enjoyment of tickling.

b The number before the trait is the rank of the correlations of that trait with ticklishness. **Bolded** names are used for traits with the strongest evidence for being an important predictor of liking to be tickled. For these traits there was an increase in ticklishness for each increase in the trait. For example, the more women liked caresses, the more they liked tickles.

ATTITUDE TO PHYSICAL CONTACT

All three traits in the category of attitude toward physical contact strongly and almost equally predicted enjoyment of tickling.

How much a woman liked tickles was strongly related to how much she liked caresses. Only 22% of the women who didn't like caresses did like tickles. That compared to 66% of the women who loved caresses. A good number of women who didn't like caresses liked tickles (the reason for this needs to be investigated further), and a third of the participants who loved caresses did not like tickles, which is less surprising but also needs further investigation.

The Percentage of Participants Who Liked Tickles According to How Much They Liked Caresses		
Liked caresses	N	Liked tickles
Very Little (1,2)	116	22%
Average (3)	140	47%
Above Average (4)	188	57%
Love It (5)	293	66%
All women	737	53%

How much the women enjoyed sex was also strongly related to how much they liked tickles. The range between the women who like sex the most and least was almost the same as it was for women who like caresses the most and least. We don't know the explanation for this relationship, but some women reported a similarity between the sensations of sex and the sensations of tickles.

The Percentage of Participants Who Liked Tickles According to How Much They Liked Sex		
Liked sex	N	Liked tickles
Very Little (1,2)	70	21%
Average (3)	160	33%
Above Average (4)	258	55%
Love It (5)	273	66%
All Participants	761	51%

We only had information about attitudes toward hugs from 270 participants. This number was sufficient to make it near certain that a relationship existed but not sufficient to precisely estimate the strength of the relationship. Of the 160 participants who had a neutral or negative attitude toward hugs, only 26% had had positive attitude toward being tickled. Of the 110 women who had a positive attitude toward being hugged, 60% also had a positive attitude toward being tickled. With more responses, we may have found a gradual increase in the percentage of liked tickling with greater enjoyment of hugs.

The Percentage of Participants Who Liked Tickles According to How Much They Liked Hugs		
Liked hugs	N	Liked tickles
Not a lot (1 To 4)	160	26%
A lot (5 to 7)	110	60%
All women	270	40%

SOCIABILITY

Two traits related to sociability predicted whether a woman likes being tickled. Women who rated themselves as likable enjoyed tickling much more often than those who saw themselves as less likable. In fact, the 46 women who rated themselves as extremely likable were more than four times as likely to enjoy being tickled as those who gave themselves a low rating. The number of participants who provided information about being likeable was small, however. Even though future studies will probably find the same relationship that we did, we doubt that it will be as strong.

The Percentage of Participants Who Liked Tickles According to Their Likability		
Rating for likeable	N	Liked tickles
Not much (1 To 3)	56	11%
Average (4)	51	28%
Above average (5 To 7)	46	46%
All women	153	27%

Women who tried to please others were also more likely to enjoy being tickled, although this connection was not as strong as that between tickling and likability.

ASSERTIVENESS

Two of the four traits in the assertiveness category were strongly related to liking to be tickled: self-confidence and winning. For women without one of those traits, the percentage who liked being ticklish was about 20%. For women with one of those traits, the percentage who like being tickled was over 40%.

The Percentage of Women Who Liked Tickles According to How They Rated Their Self-Confidence or Liking to Win				
	Self-Confidence		Liked Winning	
Rating	N	Liked tickles	N	Liked tickles
Average or below (1 to 4)	107	20%	109	21%
Above Average (5 to 7)	46	44%	44	41%
All women	153	27%	153	27%

These results differed from our expectations. We had expected that women who liked winning would not like being tickled because tickling would cause them to lose control. However, these results do fit with the observation found online that dominant women like being submissive in bed as a way to relax.

ACCEPTANCE OF RISK

Several participants suggested that liking risk would be a good predictor of liking tickling. They were correct. It could be that being tickled is a form of risk-taking in that there is a lack of control.

The Percentage of Women Who Liked Tickles According to Liking Risk		
Liked risk	N	Liked tickles
Not Much (1 to 4)	136	41%
Some to a Lot (5 to 7)	172	71%
All women	308	58%

INTELLECTUAL

Three intellectual traits were also related to enjoying tickling: analytical thinking, disliking routines, and being organized. Of the extremely analytical women, 56% enjoyed being tickled compared to only 17% of the other women. The results were similar for disliking routines and being organized.

The Percentage of Women Who Liked Tickles According to Their Analytical Thinking		
Analytical	N	Liked Tickles
Less Than Extreme (1 to 5)	114	17%
Extremely (7)	39	56%
All women	153	27%

PHYSIOLOGY

Three traits in the physiology category predicted a woman's enjoyment of being tickled. Energy and ticklishness were both strong predictors, while nervousness was a weaker predictor. Women with a high level of energy were more than three times as likely to enjoy being tickled as those with a low level of energy

(37% versus 11%). We could not determine whether it was the energetic personality type that was associated with liking tickling, or if it was simply that energetic people can accept tickling more often because they are less tired.

The Percentage of Women Who Liked Tickles According to Their Energy Level		
Energy level	N	Liked tickles
Below average (1 to 3)	61	11%
Average or higher (4 to 7)	92	37%
All women	153	27%

We also found that the greater the ticklishness, the more the women liked being tickled.

The Percentage of Women Who Liked Tickles According to Their Ticklishness Score		
Ticklish score	N	Liked tickles
None or little (1 or 2)	226	27%
Medium (3)	319	36%
Very (4)	382	52%
Extreme (5)	297	63%
All women	1224	46%

Of course, we don't know the reason why more ticklish women like being tickled more, but here are three possibilities.

1. Women who dislike being tickled make themselves less ticklish.
2. Women who dislike being tickled are tickled less and become less aware of their ticklishness.
3. For women who like being made to laugh, being more ticklish would make them laugh more.

We don't know how to reconcile the finding that more ticklish women like tickles more with the reports by some women that they don't like being tickled in their most ticklish places.

INDIVIDUAL BENEFITS OF TICKLING

Tickling can benefit both individuals and relationships. This chapter presents findings on benefits to individuals. The benefits it has for relationships will be discussed in subsequent chapters.

One individual benefiting from the tickling is of course the tickler, who gets pleasure or a feeling of power from the tickling. Some ticklees also said that they benefited because it made them laugh, created a pleasant sensation, distracted them from problems, improved their mood, relieved their stress, or increased their energy. Some women reported multiple benefits simultaneously.

THE PLEASURE OF TICKLING OTHERS

Out of 612 women, 14% did not like to tickle others, i.e., 86% did like to. The primary reason, given by 57% of the women, was to make others laugh. The next most common reason, given by 42% of the women, was to improve another's mood. Only 18% of the women liked to tickle others to annoy or punish them.

Reasons Why Participants Liked to Tickle Others (N=612)	
I don't like to tickle others	14%
To hear them laugh	57%
To improve their mood	42%
To surprise them	31%
Because it's magical that touch causes laughter	29%
To make them squirm	25%
To punish or annoy them	18%
To feel part of their body melting under my fingers	12%
Other	3%

ENJOY LAUGHING

The idea of being forced to laugh is not everybody's cup of tea, but it makes some people happier.

I mostly feel glad that I'm ticklish because it's just a very nice and memorable experience. Laughing and feeling breathless just because of a mere and pure act of tickling is really blissful.

I like tickling because it makes me laugh and when it happens, I find my body on another level. I feel happy.

I love to laugh out loud when being tickled provided it is okay in a particular situation and by familiar people.

Though the feeling of ticklish triggers me for an extreme laughter yet it feels quite good to me.

I find being able to laugh out loud and enjoy moments in life, with friends and family while being tickled.

I just enjoy the intimacy, the feeling of being out of control and forcefully made to laugh non-stop.

PLEASANT SENSATION

Another common reason that women gave for enjoying being tickled was that the sensation is pleasant. Sometimes, it was used as a form of sexual foreplay.

Surprisingly, I never feel irritated about being tickled. With the feel of tickle, goosebumps occur throughout my body that makes me feel shiver.

Being ticklish makes me glad, as whenever I am tickled, it makes me laugh like an insane and even makes my mood happier. So, to stay happy in any kind of situation, I feel glad to be ticklish. Apart from being happy, the feeling of tickle produces a sensation of sex in me which is also quite pleasurable for me. The stimulus of tickling excites my nerve with a happy feeling making me laugh louder irrespective of the situation. Though sometimes, it turns to be embarrassing, yet it gives a feeling of happiness.

It often makes me laugh and wiggle. sometimes not. but it's always a great sensation.

The types of pleasure vary. When my family tickled me it was a non-sexual feeling of euphoria. When being tickled by friends I felt pleased that I had friends who liked to make me laugh and laugh with me. When tickled by my partner the pleasure of having a friend was present along with the pleasure of that specific person's touch and how their presence feels as it interacts with mine. This last pleasure sensation is the one I usually identify as sexual.

IMPROVES MOOD

For some participants, the tickling was even more than a distraction. It was an exciting experience that transported them into a different world and gave them an excuse to let go of their inhibitions.

There is something that makes me crave tickling. An opportunity to hide all my pain and remain happy for at least some time, forgetting all the bad past and welcome good days. While being tickled, I feel like in a different world, of no worries and no sorrow.

I always felt some strange electric waves passing over my body from the site of touch that causes me to laugh hard almost unable to breathe and squirm uncontrollably. The response of my body to the touch is to get away from it immediately and to laugh. I always lost all my ability to discern what to do and just be carefree and let my body respond to it.

I believe that tickling does come up with positive vibes that can lift one's mood instantly.

You would expect women whose angry mood was made much better by tickling to like being tickled, and the vast majority did, 85%. On the other hand, some women, 19%, liked being tickled in general , even if it made their mood worse if they were tickled while angry.

The Percentage of Participants Who Liked Tickles According to How Their Mood Changes When Their Lover Tickles Them When They Are Angry		
Response to tickling	N	Liked tickles
Mood worse	192	19%
Mood unchanged	190	35%
Mood improved	204	64%
Mood much better	136	85%
All women	722	49%

DISTRACTS FROM PROBLEMS

Several women reported that tickling helped them with an emotional reset. It can break the ice and build connections.

We were having a bad time with each other due to my boyfriend's workload. I thought he ignored me. We were in a bad mood all day and were not responding to each other. And suddenly, to break the silence, he poked me on the belly. I burst into laughter at once and he got to know of it. He tickled me again and again and in no time, we, who did not even say a word to each other for the whole day, were making love. I cried out of laughter and tickling made the previously bad day, a really good day for us.

Really don't like tickling that much but if I am tickled when sad it's ok because it lightens me up.

I remember when I had a problematic boss at work, and most times, I would get home angry; tickling was one of the ways my boyfriend lightened my mood. Even though that was not all he did, he knew it was a quick way for me to become happy again.

Recently tickling helped me bond with my fiancé, helped bond us sexually and made our relationship stronger because he knows whenever I'm unhappy or sad and acting up or I'm talking too much, he just tickles me to change or lighten up my mood.

RELIEVES STRESS

Another commonly mentioned benefit of tickling was its ability to relieve stress in the same way a good run might.

The feeling when tickled is amazing. I feel at ease, and it boosts my happy hormones.

Because it makes me laugh and gives a whole new sensation in the body, I feel fresh and relaxed.

Tickling has always been a stress reliever for me, and I do it and I enjoy it most of the time.

I do get stressed most of the time for overthinking and I would thank people secretly for tickling me by surprise. I mean it's like a shot of tequila, it feels like it is a power nap or just a pause. It lessens my stress hormones.

What interests me most about tickling is the emotional stability that it brings with it. Tickling makes me laugh a lot, and as they say, laughter is the best medicine. I forget all my previous stressful situations whenever I laugh. Laughing makes me happy, thus keeping me emotionally and mentally fit and healthy.

It relaxes the body and mind. A good tickling from my boyfriend helps me relax. I get to laugh and wiggle and after that, I feel relaxed and light-weighted

The good feelings about being tickled is I laugh for certain time which makes me feel stress relief.

INCREASES ENERGY

Tickling can also increase energy like a carnival ride.

Personally, in my case, what I have found interesting about tickling is the inbuilt energy within which one can establish connections, even with strangers, provided with the people who accept it rather than getting fussed or pissed about it.

Though it is uncomfortable and makes me wiggle I feel more energetic and alive after tickled. Bad thoughts just go away. I would say it is the feeling that gives me relaxation after tickling.

I feel much bound and affiliated with my partner, because when he tickles me, I will feel more energetic, and my bonding will be increased.

THE ROLE OF TICKLING IN ADULT-CHILD BONDING

Tickling's most important role is to improve relationships: parent-child, peer, or romantic. The parent-child relationship is the least complicated; parents like to make their children laugh and most children like to be tickled, at least at a young age. For infants, the interaction is especially simple: the child initially laughs but becomes unhappy if the tickling goes on too long.

WELCOMED PARENTAL TICKLING

The reports in this study are from experiences that the women remembered when they were children. Most of the reported experiences were positive.

One of the first memories with my parents was a tickling attack! My father used to come back home after work and for some time tickling almost became a ritual for us. We used to find creative ways to get out of it as we laughed till we could not breathe—but we used to look forward to it every single evening.

When I was a young child, my parents tickled me a lot, usually because I kept laughing and thought of it as fun. As a kid, I loved being tickled by my grandparents as it was a way of them showing me their love by making me laugh. Families in India are close and live together. This closeness made me comfortable with them, and I did not mind being tickled by them.

As a young girl, my most vivid memories involve being tickled by my mother. Even though I never considered it a big part of my life in my earlier years, I realize now, years later, that tickling was a huge part of parent and child bonding and especially, between my mother and I; those moments of intense laughter and out of breath occasions are still etched in my brain.

Another memory I have of being tickled by family members is from Grandfather. I have fond memories of sitting on his lap and having him tickle the underside of my neck with his rough facial hair.

My dad is this fun type who loves spanking on me and my siblings, inviting us for a fight. Each time I ran at him for a fight, who carries me up and throws me to the chair while tickling me in the process. My mother doesn't like the idea of me laughing out loud, but I enjoyed every bit of the experience.

It reminds me of the little girl in me laughing her lungs out. It takes me down memory lane with my parents and siblings carrying me around while tickling me under my arms.

When I was a child, I loved getting tickled by an adult. I'd always run to that particular person that tickles me each time I see them, and I see them as a playmate. If anyone tickles me, they automatically become my friend.

In addition to tickling for fun, parents used tickling to distract or soothe children from anger and frustration.

My son had an online tuition class in mathematics, and he was not at all willing to do that class on that day. But I insisted him for doing the class as missing a class would make him face a serious problem in math. As I insisted, he did the class unwillingly, but he was very much angry with me. Thus, to divert his anger, I started to tickle him everywhere in his body. Though he tried to resist it for some time of his anger, yet he couldn't do it for long and started to laugh loudly. Even he started to tickle me in return and we both together laughed for a long time and thus in this way his anger for me melted just like an ice, and again the bonding between us grew sweeter than before. He apologized to me for not listening to me for a while and I have also forgiven him with a tight hug and kisses on his cheeks. This experience of tickling will be memorable for me as it helped me to build a sweeter bond with my son.

Whenever I was upset as a kid, or even today when I feel upset, my mother tickles me to make me laugh and feel better.

I associate good tickling memories to my childhood. My parents used to tickle me, especially when I'm in a bad mood. I always found it funny that I wanted to stay mad but couldn't. This, in turn, made me laugh about both the situation and tickling. I used to get some sort of inner joy and laughter somewhere from my gut. On different occasions, tickling has helped me bond with my mother. There is this particular instance when I felt broken, and she told me to cry it all out while I lied on her lap as she stroked my hair. The moment I calmed down, she made me sleep with her in the same bed. She started tickling my armpits, stomach, and neck, and all of a sudden, I started laughing as I enjoyed her tickles. I became happy and started talking about our personal lives in a friendly manner.

With my children it is quite fun to play tickle both to take away an anger, a sadness and even to convince them to carry out some activity.

My recollections of childhood experiences with tickling vary quite strongly with those of my adult years. As a child, I remember often enjoying tickling very much especially when coming from my mother. If I was in a bad mood and I was lying somewhere in a sulk, she would come over and tickle my bare feet, which invariably sent me off into a fit of giggles. This improved my mood, and my grumpiness would be forgotten. My mom respected when I had had enough of tickling and would stop the minute I asked her to.

UNWELCOMED PARENTAL TICKLING

The kind of parental tickling that was viewed positively by some children was viewed negatively by others.

Though, my mother used to tease me by gently tickling the back of my foot. At that time also, I admired that my mum is showing love to me by tickling me, so I laughed. But I resisted her as much as I can because I never enjoyed being tickled. Being tickled by friends, family members, and any other person never made me feel delighted.

CHILDREN TICKLING PARENTS

Several participants said that in their culture, it was inappropriate for children to tickle parents. However, that prohibition was not universal. In some households, parents were allowed to relax into a childlike state and show their children another side of themselves.

Many participants reported that they had tickled their own parents.

Though my mother controlled her emotions a lot, she was bound to laugh after a while on the ticklish feeling. This incident of tickling helped me to create a bond with my parents along with a sweet memory.

My best tickling experience has to be with my father. My father was a very strict person and the only way we knew to open him up was to tickle him all over and he would go crazy laughing, and more often than not, he would playfully return the favor and not stop until I started crying out of laughter.

For the longest time it has been my hobby to tickle my mother, probably because it has also been our bonding as mother and daughter. My mother is very ticklish person, imagine I am just caressing slowly her shoulders or stomach she gets really ticklish. My favorite spot to ticklish her is from her stomach and from the side of her breast. Every time I tickled her there, she laugh out loud and shout at me, almost run out of breath and almost crying from being tickled. When I tickled her so much, sometimes she got pee on her shorts and then she will get angry, but that is like for a few minutes.

Tickling also became my form of saying sorry to her, sometimes she gets frustrated and angry at me over household chores and whenever I get a chance to tickle her I will tickle her and when she react and laugh; that means we are okay again.

As we got older, the only tickling that stuck around in my family was that of my brother and me attempting to tickle my mom's feet. She's always had highly ticklish feet, and nobody was ever allowed to touch them. So, of course, that's exactly why we'd do it. She liked to unwind by watching TV in the evenings after she'd cleaned up and finished her responsibilities for the day. We'd stealthily crawl around the back of the couch, holding our breath so as not to make a sound, then we'd reach just enough of our hand up to tickle the soles of her feet with our fingertips, making sure to keep our faces out of the line of fire. Just a few quick strokes is all it took for her to scream out in surprise, kicking our hands away as we'd drop down laughing, satisfied by her reaction. This may not have been her favorite activity, but I feel that this also offered a sense of bonding. It was a playful tease that rode on the pre-established comfort we had in our relationships with our mom.

My younger sibling called to tell me my dad was angry with everyone in the house for some reason. She said sis, you ought to have been around to prevent his anger with your tickling . She knows my dad has no option than to laugh once he notices I'm going to tickle him. For that reason he always wants me to be around (and that's the bond)

I loved tickling my father when I was a kid as he is extremely ticklish and I turned it into a game to tickle him when he least expected it, when he was fixing something around the house or laying on the sofa... Sounds like torture but it was fun. I still do it sometimes.

One participant reported that her own children tickled her.

Both my children tickle me when I play with them and spend humorous time with them. Even they enjoy the sound of my laughter whenever I feel too much ticklish. Thus, while playing with my son and daughter tickling happens vice versa with a humorous response from both sides.

THE BENEFITS OF NON-SEXUAL TICKLING

Most peer tickling, especially after puberty, occurs between opposite genders. However, even when the tickling is done by romantic partners, it is often not sexual. The participants described several nonsexual benefits of tickling among peers:

- Shared laughter and silliness
- Increased energy
- Improved mood
- Reset mood after an argument
- Marked the relationship as intimate
- Was ritual play

These benefits don't radically alter lives, but they can make them more pleasant.

SHARED LAUGHTER AND SILLINESS

The most commonly reported benefit of tickling was that it provided a way to bond with a close friend through laughing and being silly together.

While we were busy ordering food, one of my friends who was sitting beside me, started to tickle me just for fun. I reacted so spontaneously that I almost fell from the chair and continued to laugh like an insane. All the people in the restaurant were looking at me. Though I understood the scenario for not to laugh, yet I could not stop myself from laughing.

I made my serious husband fall for this tickling game. So, it did help me put extra fun and happiness into my husband's mind, which is otherwise a hard task.

I had this very crazy college mate of mine, who was a good story-teller, at the same time, very clever. I still remember the first time she used this very popular trick of hers on me. She used to narrate a scary story and once I got involved in the storyline, she just tickled me on my armpits...and would laugh out loud. So, yes, this makes it clear about her crazy vibe and our bond.

Happy moments with laughter when tickled by my friends. But it is when I am younger or in my teenage years. Not in my age now that I am mother of four children. We don't have that moment what we call in tagalog is kulitan time (sweet bonding time}.

What is a relationship when the two people involved don't have fun and laugh together? One of the ways I love to have fun in my long-term romantic relationship is to tickle one another and laugh out loud.

In the long-term relationship it happened a lot while play fighting or while organizing the room together after sex or something of the sort. At this point we were very comfortable in each other's spaces, and it was always more of playfulness and fun than romantic. I feel this kind of tickling brought us closer together and increased the level of comfort we felt with each other.

Back in middle school, my friend and I used to tickle each other on the knees when we got bored. It was a lot of fun, and it would turn a boring lesson into a fun time. It was also something that only the two of us did, the others didn't like it/we just never did it to them. It is a very pleasant memory.

In my adulthood, the people I have encountered who practice tickling the most have been people who seem to value humor and laughter more than appearances. They also tend to be genuine people.

RITUAL PLAY

For some, tickling is a ritual form of play that becomes unique to a particular relationship, further increasing the bond.

Early childhood tickling within my immediate family was lovely and fulfilling, it allowed me to form bonds with my siblings and first cousins, even though at times it was done out of childhood mischief, it became an integral part of my life.

Being tickled by my lover is a very different experience when compared to the ruthlessness of my sister, and is in contrast, something that I enjoy. On the rare occasion while we are play-fighting, he will catch me off guard and tickle me under my arms or on the bottom of my feet (where I am the most ticklish!) until I beg him to stop in between laughs, and even though I squeal and try to push him off, it is still fun and makes me feel close to him. He is the only person that can ever make me ticklish now and I can't control it.

My friend turned husband. We met at my cousin's place, and we just became friends, nothing serious back then. We started going out and got to know each other better, hung out a lot. We are both very ticklish, he's even more ticklish than I am but he always tries to tickle me first and then fight back when I try to tickle him. It kinda became a game for both of us where either of us wanted to be who tickled first. Thinking about it now, it's funny how that brought us closer. Whenever we saw each other, because we lived close by, we start running, its either he's chasing me or I'm chasing him because we both know what was coming. And he always won because he was stronger and I had to always beg him to stop cos I'm literally out of breath and we will strike a deal, maybe he says, okay if I stop, you are buying me lunch or I'll take you out, which got us to spend more time together. We are both very playful people so connecting wasn't hard at all.

MARKS A CLOSE RELATIONSHIP

For some, tickling was perceived as a marker of a close relationship.

When I think about being tickled by my family, it always brings back fond memories, a show of love and connection. Similarly, this concept of tickling is very much present in the Pakistani culture, for the most part, it is considered a healthy activity that shows a strong connection between individuals and families.

My sister and I would play tickle a lot. It was a great game to us, and we loved it. We would be exhausted after but so happy.'

My siblings and I would fight and tickle each other a lot. It was a game I did kind of enjoy.

When she tickled me, I immediately felt more comfortable with her because she did something that made her feel more like family to me, since my family were the people who tickled me the most.

One woman said that there was more than laughing going on with her tickling games.

I have observed that during half of the times, someone or the other ends up farting during tickling games as it involves a lot of controlling for whatsoever.

A TABULATION OF REASONS WHY WOMEN LIKE BEING TICKLED

The above comments from the participants helped us understand why women liked being tickled. Some open-ended questions about the reasons participants liked to be tickled were asked at the beginning of the study. The answers were then listed as possible choices in multiple-response questions that allowed the women to select as many reasons as applied.

Only 15% of the women said that they never enjoyed being tickled. About half of the women said that they liked being tickled because it made them laugh. The other commonly selected circumstances were related to relationships, romantic or platonic. For some women, there may also have been physical benefits such as pleasant feelings or relaxation.

The following chart shows a tabulation of the women's responses.

Reasons Women Like Being Tickled		
Reasons	*N	% Liked
Never like	968	15%
Makes them laugh	308	51%
Sign of affection	308	45%
Helps with romance	968	44%
Helps bonding with friends	308	40%
Helps bonding with children	308	37%
Sensation pleasant	614	34%
Relaxing	308	26%
*N: Data were from 1, 2, or 3 questionnaires.		

TICKLING IN EARLY ROMANCE

The reasons for tickling and the responses to being tickled vary according to relationships. Parents don't tickle children for the same reasons that brothers tickle sisters or girlfriends tickle each other. And while boys may tickle girls purely as friends, it is often the result of sexual attraction.

The attitude about romantic tickling in this book is twofold:

1. It is not on the menu for most romantic interactions.
2. It is common enough that it could be the primary reason that humans evolved to be ticklish.

Women are well aware of the pleasure it gives men to tickle them.

My ex-boyfriend really loved the fact that I am ticklish. He told me that he was happy he could make me laugh.

I know that my boyfriend gets very excited by watching me wiggle and laugh when he tickles me.

As time went by, I experienced it as a way of flirting coming from certain men.

That does not mean, however, that all girls want to please their suitors by delivering the expected responses to his tickles.

> *I remember boys at school trying to pinch my sides or tickle me and I would feel uncomfortable. I thought it was a little nice to have some attention from the boys, but I didn't exactly like the tickling part of that. I was getting poked and pinched at work, school, and even at church. The whole thing would get pretty annoying.*

Our data show that, welcome or not, there is a whole lot of tickling going on when the relationship advances to a date. Only 19% of 916 participants had never been tickled on a date, which means that 81% of the women had been tickled by at least one person they dated.

The Number of Different Dating Partners Who Tickled the Women (N=916)	
None	19%
1 to 2	59%
3 to 5	16%
More than 5	6%

Our data also suggested that romantic tickling was probably universal. In every region we examined, at least 75% of the women had been tickled on a date. Culture apparently had very little to do with this.

The Percentage of Women Who Had Been Tickled on a Date		
	N	% Tickled
Africa	91	87%
Asia	242	74%
India 2019	137	85%
English culture	40	85%
Europe	235	79%
Latin America	91	80%
Muslim*	80	93%
All women	916	81%

*Results were skewed by a Turkish woman in the US who recruited many of her friends still living in Turkey.

INTIMACY REQUIRED FOR TICKLING

As common as tickling is in dating, it is not like telling jokes. Everyone likes a good laugh from a joke, but this study makes it clear that only a select few men, usually those romantically attached, are allowed tickling privileges.

Hugging and tickling are two different things. While people all over the world have a common, warm feeling for hugs, this is not true at all for tickles. Women have a hard time finding someone they are in sync with when it comes to tickling each other. It might take a lot of time before you find the right person but when you do, you will always have a great bond with them. To be more precise, you will bond over tickles!

Women reported that they were not receptive to tickling from men they were not attracted to. This implies that acceptance of tickling was a sign of interest in having the relationship proceed.

It is like trying the field. It happened to me all the time when I was single. When we were at the party every third guy was trying to tickle me. I didn't usually allow this. I usually accept tickling from a guy I like.

I don't allow strangers touch me even if its hugs or something like that. That's why I allow to tickle and touch me only people I know or like a lot.

She said that a friend who liked her would try to tickle her just to touch her, and she didn't like it because it felt sleazy, not fun.

Whenever I am tickled, there is usually (if not always) a sense of fear that shows up along with the feeling of pleasure and laughter. I think this may be why I get angry or annoyed when I am tickled by people I do not want to tickle me or when I do not want to be tickled. Since the more pleasurable feelings do not appear during those moments, it feels more like an unwanted attack and I am inclined to move away and yell.

Even recently I experienced and went through a series of emotions and thoughts when a male colleague of mine tried to tickle me. It just does not make me feel comfortable at all. So, I think for guys other than partners, it's better that they keep themselves away from not initiating such acts, or else would even end up not having that friendship again.

On the other hand, for women in a committed romantic relationship, tickling by lovers could be a joyful experience.

During my adolescence the ticklers were my friends and my boy-friend. I hated when my friends used to tickle me, but I loved when my boyfriend used to do it.

I feel loved and pampered when my boyfriend tickles me. The feel-ing is totally different from what I experience with others. I can admit that I enjoy being tickled only when my boyfriend does it. When he tickles me, I love the sensation and the feeling of being tickled. I don't feel uncomfortable with his touch or tickling.

One reason for the pleasure of tickles may be that is sexu-ally stimulating if the woman is already sexually attracted to the tickler.

I am a very ticklish person, but it could only get sexual IF I know the person that touches my weak spots would be 'the man' I am committed to, not with just anyone who will just touch or tickle me.

As a ticklish woman, I love it when my lover tickles me. With my friends, every tickle helps me to connect with them, but it is dif-ferent with my lover. Whenever he tickles me, my body resumes to a state of submission.

Tickling can be sexually stimulating or annoying, depending on who is doing the tickling. If my boyfriend does it, it can be tick-lish{and} can cause good sensations that can sometimes lead to sexual stimulation.

The above comments suggest that women don't welcome just any tickler. That is supported in spades by the results from the structured questionnaires. Of the 287 women who answered one questionnaire, 59% considered it at least somewhat creepy when a male friend tickled them during a conversation. No doubt, it would be close to 100% of women tickled by males who were not their friends.

In a different dataset of 510 women, we also found that 59% of the women would not allow even a close male friend to tickle them. Forty-seven percent had to be dating or considering sex for the tickling to be okay, and for 13%, not even considering sex was enough. The bottom line is that most women consider tickling to be an intimate interaction.

Feelings About Male Friend Who Tickles You (N=287)	
1 (Very creepy)	21%
2	17%
3	21%
4 (Neutral)	18%
5	11%
6	7%
7 (Very fun)	5%

Intimacy Required for Tickling by a Male (N=510)	
Friend	8%
Close friend	33%
Dating	25%
Considering sex	22%
Never okay	13%

PUBERTY AND TICKLISHNESS

Puberty may change the nature of tickling in different ways. One way is that it may increase ticklishness.

> *As I grew up my body also grew with me and there come other parts which become more ticklish than my stomach and underarms, and these parts includes my breasts, navel, between legs.*

More importantly, puberty added a sexual component to the sensation of tickling.

> *When 15 I can say that I have been more ticklish now than when I was 18. I have noticed it since I started going out with my first date. I believe there are some kind of feeling that when we are touched or tickled by the one that we intimately want, our body quickly responds to it in a form of arousal, and that's how I perceived tickling now that I am an adult.*

That sexual component was easily elicited by tickling in some women.

> *It comes to the opposite gender or someone whom I think has a liking towards me, when they tickle or even touch me, I get sexual feelings and all sorts of doubts in my mind.*

> *When I was young, probably a school-going kid, I think I used to feel very mischievous about the act of tickling. While I was a teenager, tickling on my body parts other than my face used to give me more sexual feelings, especially if it's a guy doing it to me.*

When I am tickled in a dating relationship, I mostly enjoy the excitement of feeling ticklishness as that tends towards the sexual feeling.

When a classmate that I was attracted to or liked more was doing it {tickling}, a sexual tension was also building up in me whether I wanted to acknowledge that or not. But also, it was the period when my hormones exploded, I was becoming a woman and an abundance of new experiences and feelings filled every inch of my body. This being one of them.

Several women mentioned that the sensation of tickling was their introduction to sexual sensation.

When I was a teenager, I started to have new experiences with tickling. It started when my friends used to tickle me in the sides, I noticed that now tickling not just made me laugh but I have started to feel something different, these sensations were very new to me back then. And sometimes I could even get these sensations whenever I used to touch myself in a certain way. I used to enjoy these sensations back then and I still do. At fifteen I was introduced to a new kind of tickle. My boyfriend was ready to move forward with our relationship and he decided to make a move while he was kissing me. The backs of fingers brushed my breast, it sent a tingling tickle through me, what I now understand as a sensual tickle. At that time, I got to know how tickling at certain parts started giving me sexy feelings. A year later I met a guy that was a bit older than me and was a lot more experienced, he used a feather on my neck, down my ribs and on the inside of my thigh, showing me that sensual tickles can actually take your breath away and make you weak in the knees.

As we sat on a couch in a relatively private corner of the patio, enjoying another glass and watching the moonlight reflect off the waves, he gently placed his hand on my knee and slowly, lightly brushed his fingertips up and around my leg, creating a tickling sensation that quickly turned to heightened sensitivity and arousal throughout my body. I had never felt that way before, and it undoubtedly made me curious and excited for more.

When I was young and innocent, tickling always made me laugh. After turning 18 and beyond, tickling for me means something personal. My body can't control the feeling, but it will matter more on who is doing it.

He tickled me with the tip of his fingers at this point. Note that before this tickling incident, we were simply pals, and though I was used to getting attacked with tickles by my family, my heart skipped a beat. It was the first time I felt the tingling sensation that comes with being attracted to the opposite sex.

I was sure that we were just friends. You know that innocent kind in which you walk in the park, exchange music preferences, and gossip about other kids. One day, I stole this boy's cap and didn't want to give it back. So, he grabbed me by my waist and started to tickle me to make me return it. Those tickles made me feel something I've never felt before. My body was still moving involuntary, and I was still laughing out loud. Yet, there was also a heat I was not familiar with.

The first time my partner tickled my sides, I was instantly startled and frantically moved my body to get away. But as we got more intimate, my feelings towards being tickled changed.

On the other hand, the sexual nature of tickling can diminish with further sexual maturity and experience.

As I grew older, my body and its sensors changed. At that point, the simple and innocent tickling gesture didn't arouse me anymore. But the gentle movement on my skin from my partner or his tickling breath did.

MAKING RELATIONSHIPS MORE PHYSICAL

There were several reports of how tickling advanced the sexual nature of a relationship. For those without sexual experience, tickling may be used to overcome anxiety about intimate touch. It provides the wannabe lover a way to test the waters for physical availability or provides an excuse for more intimate contact. It acts as a Trojan horse for laying on hands. You were tickled all the time when you were a kid. What's the big deal?

The most precious and heartwarming memory of us for me would be the day he proposed to me to be his girlfriend. He came to me and told me that we were going to his house for doing the projects that we were assigned. To my surprise, he had balloons hung up, a rose in his hand and a big smile on his face. Because of our bickering friendship I thought he was pulling a prank on me and did not react to the setting. But then he lifted me up, placed me on the couch and started tickling me. He reached out his hand on my belly then on my neck, then the tickling war began. We tickled each other until we were tired. But then we got into a loving relationship.

Although initially, we had starting troubles to reach private parts, we could do it smoothly through the act of tickling and then getting used to it.

We were quite afraid to even look at each other then, because of how teachers perceived communications among boys and girls to be only for the love and lust part of it. But we did spend good times in the Tuition center, after the Tuition classes, while walking back home. I still remember how we used to wrap his hands on my waist affectionately and then tickle me to laughter. There were even times, while he slid his hands through my t-shirt and tickled me on my tender belly, which felt super fun and romantic.

We weren't best of friends or close to each other from the first day. We started out as just regular friends, he found out about how ticklish I am and lol he made it a thing that he had to find me every day and tickle me so he would get a chance to make me laugh every day. And just like that, we saw each other every day and our feelings grew stronger and here we are today.

From several comments, tickling seemed to be more part of the male than female arsenal.

From my relationship and that of my friends I have observed that it's usually the guy who comes up with the tickling. So tickling while in a relationship starts as a fun act, which majority of the time also has sexual intentions when the partners are comfortable around.

For guys, I think trying to tickle their partner in the initial stage of relationships, gives them a kickstart and to know if the girl is comfortable about the touchy things or not. Also, for girls while in relationship it's moreover a romantic act than a fun act I feel.

Collateral benefits of tickling may also be helpful.

Tickling while in a relationship adds in romantic eye contacts which can often be a start to foreplay.

Tickling makes a physical relationship easier for both girls and boys.

Tickling while in a relationship always helps to enhance the mood and make it more pleasurable. It just gives a start to the remaining things. Not just for the girl, I think it also helps the guys to ease out and to start getting comfortable with the girl.

After the relationship has advaned, however, tickling is less necessary as an excuse for physical contact.

And to compare, in my relationship where we have often got physical the frequency of tickling is comparatively less when taking the case of my friend who just recently started dating. So for them, it's mostly these fun acts and play which is more as they are yet to get started with other physical stuff I guess. But for me at the same time, the frequency of normal tickles from my boyfriend has decreased when compared to the initial times, as now we are more comfortable with each other and require less ice-breakers before initiating stuff.

GATEWAY TO FIRST SEXUAL EXPERIENCE

Tickling can undoubtedly act as a transition towards more intimate forms of touch; it even took some relationships to the finish line.

As there was nobody in his house, we went there to spend quality time. After entering his house, I went and sat in his living room. He went to the kitchen to serve me some drinks and snacks. While he was pouring juice into the glass, I went to the kitchen and hugged him tightly. Then he turned around and started to tickle me around my neck region and even kissed all over my neck. I felt highly ticklish, and goosebumps were created throughout my body. However, for this stimulus, a sensation of sex grew all over my body. Looking at my sensitive reaction, my ex-lover continued to tickle me sensitively throughout my body. In that situation, we both intensively felt to do sex and so we shifted to his bedroom. Thus, we continued to do sex for a long time by satisfying both of our intent for the first time.

I have a very funny experience of my first sex with my then boyfriend, who is my husband now. Our first sexual date began with a funny tickling experience. Before becoming lovers, we were very good college friends and from then onwards he knew that I have a weakness towards the feeling of ticklishness and so he attempted to tickle me for long on that date. When my boyfriend proposed me for the first sexual date, I felt very shy and was quite timid for the first-time sex with my boyfriend. Though I had a desire for that, yet I felt too shy. Although we began the date with complete romance and he gradually started to come closer to me for indulging in the sexual meet. But, as I was feeling too shy, I avoided him with all my sweetness. So, he started to tickle me to divert my attention. Out of extreme ticklishness I kept running all around the room and entered into the bathroom. My boyfriend also entered there chasing me and from getting rid of him, I fell into the bathtub, where I had no way to escape and then there, we had our first sex accompanied with sweet smiles and laughter.

We were playing a video game. When my boyfriend saw himself losing the game, he started tickling on my waistline so that I may lose control and he succeeded. Putting the game controller aside, I started leaning due to that sensation and he got above me, and we started making love.

There was this day, I went out on a date with a guy, it was at a nature park, the weather was cool and all, at first, I felt so somber trying to take a deep breath, close my eyes and enjoy the beauty of nature but the guy would not have it, he started tickling my ribs to get me into an excited mood and it worked for him.

Tickling was reported as a useful tool even for newly married couples who had been chaste before the ceremony.

After freshening up ourselves we both started to discuss our honeymoon when suddenly my husband pulled me closer to him and started to tickle me around my abdomen and even kissed there, which is quite a sensitive area for feeling ticklish. Thus, I started to feel highly ticklish along with the feeling of heavenly pleasure that was induced in me. Therefore, gradually we both got indulged in the sexual activity that drove us to another beautiful world with immense smoothness and pleasure. That night we had the best sexual and romantic experience that initiated with tickle. Thus, we would never forget our first wedding night throughout our life and would always remain special to us.

On my wedding night, I was very nervous. Apart from being very tired from the entire ceremony, I was worried about having sex with my husband. This feeling was my first time and being intimate with a long-time friend come husband. As we sat on the bed revisiting the events of the day, I wished we would talk ourselves to sleep. Nobody knew how to start, and if it was supposed to flow, the current was stuck somewhere far from us. However, God did whisper some wisdom into his ears as the thought of tickling me came to his mind. Well, he suggested how he would make me relax, and I gave in. The delicate light touches made me relax. Well, this relaxation made one thing lead to many others, and my wedding night turned out sweet, sensational and memorable thanks to tickling.

USEFUL APHRODISIAC

While not necessarily sexual in nature, tickling can serve as an aphrodisiac if the woman is already attracted.

Since I became sexually active, tickling has become a sexual blessing. Tickling is the best way to set up the mood of my partner and mine as well. Even apart from sexual experiences

There was this incident when I had to crash in with a random guy during a college fest.. We found out that we had very similar tastes and we played one of our favorite songs and were casually dancing to the song, when grabs my waist and tickles me. {The situation} felt romantic and slowly got me in the mood for sex., but we didn't have contraceptives so we had to drop the idea but God, that was one absolute best memory of how important a role tickles can play to get your sex drive strong.

My lover took me to a cottage that was booked for us and started to tickle me around my neck and hip area. I felt quite ticklish and there were goosebumps throughout my body and even a sensation of sex grew in me. Thus, on feeling the sensation of sex, we both were indulged in the sexual activity that brought pleasure to our mind and soul.

I find it sensual foreplay. I love doing it to my partner and them to me. It definitely enhances the desire and anticipation.

My boyfriend knows tickling me is a gateway to getting laid.

In addition to being inherently sexually stimulating, the laughter and playfulness it induces can promote relaxation.

Like I said, laughing with your partner can be a huge sexual stimulant for some people. It is for me. Laughing openly, in a playful manner can help release all the nervousness (if any), alleviate insecurities and make the mood lighter.

Being around him made me horny in many weird ways. For us, tickling was always followed by flirting, and it would become a playful touch until we get sexual.

Tickling helps promote sex by increasing play that can lead to sex.

The feeling is pleasant especially during lovemaking. I enjoy my lover's tickles during sex. So, it's true the pleasant sensation of tickles enhances sexual experience. Also, it relaxes the body and mind. A good tickling from my boyfriend helps me relax. I get to laugh and wiggle and after that, I feel relaxed and light-weighted.

The laughter caused by the tickling had special benefits for some men.

The last time we had sex which was the first time I've been tickled during sex, he said he enjoyed it more when I giggle during tickling, and it feels good.

TICKLING WITH LONG-TERM PARTNERS

The previous chapter was about the significant role that tickling can play in beginning and cementing a relationship. Of course, its role in maintaining a long-term relationship may be at least as important.

SHOWS AFFECTION

Tickling does more than spice up sex; it can strengthen a relationship through multiple forms of connection. One of the simplest reasons why women seem to enjoy it is because it shows affection. Like other playful, intimate gestures such as hugging, nudging, and kissing foreheads, tickling is a close and physical, yet non-invasive way for someone to express their affection for another.

I was very nervous because I had a bad day at the work which immediately changed the situation between our family. After some time, my son came up to me and we were cuddling and talking and at some point he started to sing a song and tickle me. There is one song for tickling in our city (probably even on the whole Balkan region) which I'm not sure if I can tell you on English, but you are supposed to sing it and at the end to tickle a person whenever you know she is ticklish. So, he started tickling me on the side, of course

I knew what would happen, so I wasn't really feeling the tickling, but still I was smiling. I was smiling more because of him, and his way of showing me that he cares for my happiness. I also think that tickling can be good way to show someone that you love them.,

Whenever we are at home, my lover tickles me randomly. I might be by the sink, and he would just pass by and tickle me. I would laugh out loud before continuing with my chores. Those are one of the sweetest memories I have in relationships; the random tickle that shows affection.

There is a different feeling when my boyfriend tickles me, it's relaxing and appealing, calling and showing love and affection.

I love it when my lover tickles me, it shows much affection, playfulness and a sense of familiarity with me.

HELPS BONDING

Tickling can't solve fundamental problems, but it can help surmount problems on a temporary basis. For starters, it can help someone overcome feelings of anger.

Our secret to a healthy and happy relationship became tickling. Whenever we got into a fight, we would tickle each other and release off all of our tension. Tickling really helped in mutual understanding between us and deepen our bond.

While I used to tickle with my husband after marriage as I experienced this sort of tickling. He used this first time to give me pleasure and release my anger. Suddenly I felt well and my anger was gone.

It can also distract someone from other problems.

I really like being ticklish because it strengthens the bond that we have with my partner. We momentarily forget our problems every time we tickle each other. It's a quick escape from reality.

When I'm pissed and my partner caresses my sensitive areas, it makes me feel giddy, and I laugh. This changes my mood in a positive way, except when I'm too mad.

Unfortunately, tickling is not the magic touch that solves all conflicts. Without effort at understanding, it can make problems worse.

I had a fight with boyfriend. I was angry and he tried to calm me or to make that intense gone. But I was pissed off by that tickling. Instead of talking seriously he irritated me with pathetic trying of tickling.

When both participants are on the same page, tickling can make for good play.

He'd always try for the knees while I exclaimed something like who's even ticklish on their knees? I'd act tough, like he couldn't break me, but then he'd tickle the back of my thigh, and I'd lose control. It was fun, a form of play, and I recognize it now as a way for us to bond as well.

It can also act as a one-two punch of first play and then sex.

One Sunday evening I was sitting on the bed by the window and my husband was having tea. He comes up to me after finishing his cup and rubs my neck with his thumb saying the tea was good. I say that's for always so he pinches me softly and I pinch him back and this turns into a tickle fight in not more than a minute. I was just wondering how to spend the evening and then we had that beautiful thing going on, I was almost winning over him when he got a bit too hard and tickled me till I had to move my face away for air. I looked out of the window, breathed in deeply and before I could even turn back properly, he grabbed my nape and started tickling back while making sure I was okay. We were laughing our lungs out after a long time — it got sensual and gradually put us both in a sexual mood. In fact, making someone laugh and caring for them unconditionally is a big turn on for both of us so the ticking just played right.

One time we were home on a weekend, and we were talking and the next thing we started our usual tickle fight/play which he always wins but sometimes lets me win. So that day while we were tickling each other and laughing, I was getting turned on at the same time, i also noticed he was getting turned on too, we started kissing and the next thing we just jumped right into tearing each other's clothes off and having sex. This is a very common scenario in my house. We are both very ticklish, we are in love, and we play a lot so any little body touch or tickle arouses both of us. It is magical.

It's also a one-two punch that works for turning anger management into make-up sex.

After marriage when my husband promised me, he will be picking me up for a movie. But that not happened anyway and I'm in such a sad and angry face exposing in front of him. Just imagine how he could excuse that when it comes to our first outing. I was not talking to him at all. That was the first time he started tickling me. First, I tried to escape and wiggled but later I started to laugh, and all my evil spirit went out so easily. And then we made love.

TICKLING AS COMMUNICATION

Some couples use tickling to signal that they want sex or to evaluate their partner's current desire for it. The act allows couples to bridge awkward barriers in communication and create a mood that's both playful and erotic.

My boyfriend and I often start with tickling, like sending a signal there is possibly for having sex. I remember moments when we were in bed just talking, and then from nowhere he starts tickling me just for fun. But this simple and innocent fun makes me prepared for the sex.

He always tickles me when he wants to have sex but feels like I'm tense, nervous or too tired. Despite of my bad mood, if he tickles me, it is pretty much enough to change the whole mood.

Being the communicative person in our relationship, my partner is the exact opposite of who I am. I have come to realize that tickling is his love language whenever he is in the mood for sex. He is a shy person. He struggles to communicate his feelings directly to me, but with a tickle, I can tell all the things he wishes to do to me.

We use it in foreplay. Sometimes it's to get each other in the mood and turn each other on so it turns from play to something more. It's a good tester to see if the other is in the mood actually.

My partner has tickled me to initiate sex. He'll also tickle me a bit in the foreplay stages of our intimacy, usually to indicate the desire, then sometimes in a slightly more aggressive and playful manner as we're taking off our clothes.

PLEASES PARTNER

A woman's ticklishness may not attract men as much as her face, body, or personality, but for some men, it's in the mix of sexually pleasing attributes. Several women reported that their ticklishness gave their partner pleasure.

I am happy when my partner likes to play with me and touch me in a certain way to see me laughing or enjoying (in bed).

If I laugh and wiggle on being tickled, then it surely sexually excites my partner.

Tickling with my romantic partner is always pleasing to both of us. I like being tickled by him because it arouses him quickly, and he stays in that state during the entire sexual intercourse. As he tickles me, we both remain lustful for each other longer.

It makes me feel like I am not in control of my body and that I have surrendered it to him to do whatever he likes, and I am happy about it.

With my partner, there are times I can let him tickle me even if it's uncomfortable. Why? Because I know he will tickle me in many other places that will give me more pleasure, making me forget the irritation.

I'm happy about the fact that I'm ticklish for my partner.

TICKLING AS PART OF FOREPLAY

In the previous sections, we provided evidence that tickling smooths the path to a physical relationship. In this section, we show that it is sexually arousing in both the early and later stages of foreplay. It may contribute to playfulness, laughing, wiggling, relaxing, bonding, and heightened sensation.

I must say it did help with sexual life. It's one way to start sexual game, to prepare each other to the intercourse. It makes sex more pleasant. It makes me relaxed. It definitely makes partner ready for the sex. It reduces intense if there is one.

I feel ticklish when he inserts hand between legs, and I laugh then he happily tickles on my toes and around thighs. It improves our feelings to sex.

The sensation of tickling sometimes overlaps with the sexual sensation.

I was not in that mood at that time. Above all, my husband knew how to create my mood. So, he started to tickle me around the sensitive areas of my body to create the sensation of sex. After tickling me for some time, when I started to feel the sensation of sex and got in the full mood to do the same, we started to enjoy our anniversary night with a wonderfully romantic and loving experience, which on remembering, still leaves an impression of romance in our mind.

Due to the pandemic situation we arranged a private party at our house. While dancing late at night suddenly, my husband tickled sensually on my back and around my lower hip region. I felt so ticklish that I spontaneously reacted with shivering throughout my body. With the ticklish feeling, I hugged him tightly, and thus the mood for sex triggered within me. Moreover, understanding the situation my husband continued to tickle me more throughout my body along with the sexual parts that influenced us to do more sex for a long time.

Between me and my husband. I get tickles in the most vulnerable spots of my body which I believe sends a signal to my brain that is similar to feelings with an orgasm. Knowing the weak spots of each other's body, my husband and I tend to attack each other randomly as a 'flirting' stage before it leads to sex.

Elaborate tickling games may set the table for sex. They are both playful and arousing.

My friend Divya was telling us about a new way she found the long-lost spark in her relationship. She and her husband were playing a game of truth and dare, that is when a dare showed up and asked them to see which one of them was the most ticklish. Her husband went first. He wasn't responding as she had expected. When it was her turn to get tickled, she knew she had already lost. She said that she was very ticklish in her neck and side breasts; that is where her hubby attacked the most. The next moment she got so turned on that she led him to the bed. It led to some very passionate sex. She also mentioned that her hubby found it pleasing when he tickled her in private and intimate areas.

In terms of sex, tickling as foreplay is one of the ways I would say is helpful in getting more intimate and physical with my partner. Especially when on the bed, tickling fights are mostly done when either partner can position themselves on the other and gain dominance.

When prior to sexual intercourse, there is a game where tickling is included, and they arrive to relax the moment and then move on to the act as such.

If it's during foreplay, being tickled would make me feel safe, relaxed, and above all, sexually excited.

Some ticklish areas serve as erogenous zones.

There are some specific parts in my body which on tickled get me in the mood for sex. These are the areas around the lower hip portion, around the back, in and around the breast, and around the bikini area.

So, he started to tickle me around the sensitive areas of my body to create the sensation of sex. After tickling me for some time, when I started to feel the sensation of sex and got in the full mood to do the same, we started to enjoy our anniversary night with a wonderfully romantic and loving experience, which on remembering, still leaves an impression of romance in our mind. Thus, similar to the anniversary night, a few more times, we had a pleasing and loving sexual experience that was started through the feeling and sensation of tickling.

Tickling arouses me — yes. It is one of the ways to get ready for the sex. When I am laying in the bed or doing something he comes quietly from the back and starts with my neck. He tickles with his lips. Oh, it arouses me a lot.

For example, I sometimes experience both types of tickling on my butt. When my boyfriend is aggressively trying to tickle me to make me laugh, the butt is one of the few spots that will really get me. However, I also find it extremely arousing when my butt is tickled during foreplay. I know he loves to touch and play with it, so although it is immediately sensitive {to tickling} , it's also quite a turn-on to me. When we're in that mode, I become more attentive to the other sensations that the tickle triggers rather than reactive to the initial sensitivity.

When tickled on the breasts, they stand erect and sensitive even with a little touch. On the arms and thighs, I get goosebumps and my muscles twitch at times. Being tickled on the inner thighs makes my legs shake uncontrollably as well. On the neck region and in the ears, tickling makes me laugh and I end up feeling a weakness I cannot even explain when with my romantic partner.

My butt, back of legs and neck are great spots to tickle if you want to get down with me and this guy is just the best at it. He slowly tickles the back of my legs and that's like the introduction to the foreplay, then while he's kissing me, he tickles my neck at the same time and the feeling is that of both giggling and arousal. He's very patient with my body and he knows how to work it, just the right amount to turn me on and not make me laugh out loud.

The tickling sensation can enhance the sexual sensations.

So yes, I enjoy being tickled while having sex, but mostly when it's done to increase sensitivity during foreplay.

Of course, timing is important.

While a playful tickle can be a fun way to initiate sex, that ticklish feeling becomes less pleasant as sensation throughout the body is increased and more pleasurable feelings arise.

With experience, some of the women became connoisseurs of tickling. They learned where, how long, and how hard they had to be tickled to experience the full intensity of the arousal that it can induce.

I experience pleasure when tickled gently and not continuously. What do I mean by this? Instead of tickling me non-stop, I prefer him tickling me for a second, pausing for a second, and then continuing with the cycle as this makes me want to have sex immediately.

DURING INTERCOURSE

As well as being arousing, tickling also enhances the sexual sensation after penetration for some women.

The sensation of tickling in me always makes our sexual experience better, and so my husband most of the time starts tickling me for enjoying a better sexual pleasure. That evening we kept on doing sex for complete three hours and I could get into my conscience only when I heard the cry of my daughter from the next room.

In the lights of my personal experiences, tickling is a best way of enhancing sexual pleasure. Each and every time, when we started sexual activities with tickling, it made us more closure and bonded with each other. And very much noticeably our relation changed towards more sexual from less sexual or non-sexual. And even in the duration of sexual relation, it also made a phenomenal change. I feel more happy, bonded and sexual pleasure in the result of tickling. This not only my case, it's similar to my husband as well. Whenever we come closure to each other without tickling, he always mentions that today something we are missing, and we feel less sexual and pleasure.

When I am tickled during the intercourse session, I get more indulged in the intercourse with desire for more sex from my partner.

Sometimes, even after he was inside me, he would tickle under my arms or my neck, and it would help me have an orgasm. Sometimes he would tickle my feet when we were having oral sex. I would not enjoy sex as much without that tickling. The feelings that I get

*when I'm tickled make sex much better for me. I would hate it if
I were not ticklish.*

One woman found that tickling made her comfortable and
allowed her to better enjoy a sexual experience. For her, the
intimacy that came from tickling became the most important
part of sex.

*Does tickling enhance my sexual experience? Yes, it does. In a very
soothing way. It kind of makes sex more complete, and affection-
ate. For me it doesn't have to be just sex, some feelings should be
added to make it more intimate and romantic, and that's what
tickling does, otherwise, I don't get comfortable. This is how it
helps enhance my sexual experience. My partner noticed I was very
difficult (not comfortable), and not interested when it comes to sex
(because I don't enjoy sex), and to help enhance the experience, he
needs to tickle and caress during sex.*

Some men get excited by the responses of the women to tickling.

*If I laugh and wiggle on being tickled, then it surely sexually excites
my partner i.e., my husband, as he jumps off on me with the desire
for sex and continues to kiss me on several parts of my body.*

*While being tickled on the bed, I guess it gives me that naughty
laugh that my boyfriend enjoys.*

*As I laugh and wiggle on being tickled, my partner does take it as a
positive signal that I am enjoying it, and it simply encourages him
to do more, which has simply enhanced our sex life.*

My husband knows how ticklish I am. He discovered that when we made love on the night of our wedding day. When he held my waist and pulled toward him, I wiggled and got tickled. As I asked my husband about this, he finds it attractive and funny as well.

As my husband says that during wiggling and laughing when I am tickled is exciting for him. As, he enjoys my voices, and changing facial expressions, which makes him more aroused and happy.

I do believe that laughing and wiggling both make me appealing to my current partner, and I believe the answer would be the same for those who have tickled me in the past. Furthermore, the eagerness of my partner to tickle me regularly tells me that he's largely doing it for his own pleasure. Although the playful nature of our dynamic certainly makes it a shared activity, my feelings about being tickled fluctuate with my mood, while his seem to remain consistent. For this reason, I believe that he tickles me more because he enjoys the interaction than specifically to give me pleasure.

He said it like a passive comment/joke that when he's inside me and I giggle, he feels it in his penis and he likes it.

Yes, I believe just like how men enjoy hearing the sexual moans, they also enjoy women's reaction to tickles.

While almost all the women described experiences in heterosexual relationships, it was also reported as an important part of the sexual relationship of one lesbian couple.

I am very ticklish, my partner knows this, I'm gay but I can't be very open about it here in Nigeria so we pretend we are best friends. We met at a party, clicked almost immediately, she touched my thighs and found out I was ticklish and we made a joke about it. I told her I'm very ticklish and she asked me what I thought about being tickled as part of sex and I was like nah that's weird but she told me not to worry and just tell her the most sensitive parts of my body. I did and she tickled me like she knew my body and my body responded like it knew her hands. It was funny because I was laughing and getting turned on at the same time. We have incorporated it in our sex life and it's great, the tickling is great, the sex is great too... She's a wonderful partner and she understands my body and makes it respond to her tickles.

Although tickling often helps with foreplay, several women found tickling during intercourse an unpleasant distraction.

The thing about tickling and how I relate it to sexual pleasure or arousal is that if I'm tickled by the right person, it turns me on. I won't say it has helped me achieve orgasm because I don't like being tickled during sex. It's like a foreplay thing for me and I get goosebumps when it's really good.

I don't like being tickled after penetration. My partner doesn't tickle me during sex because he knows I don't like it during sex.

I don't like that (being tickled after penetration). I prefer the sensitive spots to be touched during sex.

THE FREQUENCY OF TICKLING DURING INTERCOURSE

Women reported that they were frequently tickled during foreplay and after penetration. During foreplay, 52% of 602 women said that they were tickled sometimes, frequently, or usually. That number was reduced to 35% after penetration. In a group of 303 women, 54% of the women were tickled sometimes, frequently, or usually during sex, without specifying whether it was during foreplay or after penetration. These results show that tickling has a role in sex for a large number of women but is not frequently part of sex for the majority of women.

| Frequency of Being Tickled During Sex | | |
	During foreplay N=602	After penetration N=586	Not specified N=303
Never	27%	40%	26%
Rarely	20%	25%	20%
Sometimes	27%	23%	32%
Frequently	14%	9%	13%
Usually	11%	3%	9%

In almost all regions surveyed, more than half of the women were sometimes tickled during sex. The exception was Europe, which included mostly women in Eastern Europe. We also found evidence that Africans may experience more tickling during sex than women in other regions. What is clear from the data is that tickling during sex is not rare in any region studied.

The Percentage of Women Sometimes Tickled During Sex		
	N	
Africa	86	70%
Asia	238	62%
India 2019	137	61%
English culture	39	59%
Europe	233	30%
Latin America	88	51%
Muslim	78	60%
Total	899	53%

WOMEN'S RESPONSES TO LOVER'S TICKLING

If the tickling came from their lover, 56% of 321 women enjoyed at least the first few seconds.

How Do the First Few Seconds of Being Tickled by Your Lover Feel to You (N = 321)	
Unpleasant	8%
Tolerable	36%
Good	56%

In another data set of 740 women, 24% of the women usually enjoyed being tickled by their romantic partner, and another 21% frequently enjoyed it. We assume from these numbers that tickling often has a positive effect on bonding in romantic relationships.

Frequency of Enjoying Tickling by Romantic Partner (N=740)	
Rarely	18%
Sometimes	37%
Frequently	21%
Usually	24%

Nearly half, 47%, of 760 women surveyed, reported that their partner's tickling made their mood better when they were angry. However, tickling was certainly not a reliable cure for bad moods in all women; 27% reported that it made a bad mood either somewhat worse or much worse.

How Does Tickling by Your Romantic Partner Affect Your Mood When You Are Angry? (N=760)	
Much worse	12%
Somewhat worse	15%
No effect	26%
Somewhat better	29%
Much better	18%

FREQUENCY THAT TICKLING IMPROVED SEX

From the reports above, we know that tickling can improve sexual experiences. We used the analysis of responses to multiple-choice questions to evaluate how often that happens. Of the 261 women who answered the question, 30% said that their sexual experience had been improved many times or several times by tickling.

Has Tickling Improved Your Sexual Interactions with Your Lover? (N=261)	
Many times	18%
Several times	12%
A few times	40%
Almost never	30%

Another question given to a different set of 223 participants asked about the effect of tickling on their sexual experiences. When the question was asked this way, 64% said that it made their sexual experiences better (33% said that tickling made them much better, and 31% said that it made them some better). One possible explanation of the sharp differences in these results is that tickling was not often part of sex for women, but when it was used, it made the experiences better. Without further data, we would guess that tickling is a useful part of sex for 25% of women because that is the percentage that is frequently tickled during sex and for whom sex has been improved many times.

Effect of Tickling on Sexual Experiences N=223	
Much worse	2%
Some worse	4%
Little effect	30%
Some better	31%
Much better	33%

Although tickling probably enhances sex for a substantial number of women, it may also ruin sex. When asked how frequently their partner ruined sex by tickling them, 21% of the women claimed this happened frequently or usually. These results suggest that at least some men enjoy tickling their partners during sex, even if the women don't like it.

Frequency Partner Ruins Sex by Tickling (N= 463)	
Never	37%
Rarely	24%
Sometimes	18%
Frequently	16%
Usually	5%

You will have noticed by this time that we have definitively answered the age-old question, "What do women want?" The answer, of course, is that it all depends. There are a large number of women who benefit from tickling in their romantic relationships and a large number who don't. It will be a long time before AI can predict who and when. In the meantime, we have to rely on communication.

PREFERRED SPOTS TO BE TICKLED DURING SEX

The response to tickling varied greatly based on the location of the tickle. Sites for tickling could be chosen for several reasons, including the type of sensation at that site, the ease of access during sex, whether or not it's an erotic location, and the woman's degree of ticklishness. Naturally, some women were less particular than others and liked any kind of tickling during sex.

I love getting tickled during sex, irrespective of the place. Simply put, I love being tickled on my breasts, my neck, my inner thighs and around my vagina, especially near my clitoris and my peri-neal raphe.

However, the impression given by the data is that most women have preferences for where they are tickled during sex.

There are some specific parts in my body which on tickled get me in the mood for sex. These are the areas around the lower hip portion, around the back, in and around the breast, and around the bikini area.

Like most girls in my village, I became sexually active when I was 14. At that time tickling became very sexual for me. When my boyfriend tickled any part of my body, but especially my belly button and vagina, I would get very aroused and want to have sex with him.

I am most ticklish at the back my ears. That brings up my body heat and turns me on

The favorite part of my body for my husband to tickle is the back of the ear and neck, but the neck is my favorite. I don't like him tickling my foot because I know it's dirty.

As my dating became more intimate and I began having longer term partners where we would experiment more, I discovered I liked sensual tickling a lot. They would avoid the ribs because that was a turn off, but I liked it on a lot of other areas of my body. Not stroking! I don't want to feel like an animal being petted. I like soft, light tickling where your fingers move.

The preferred sites for being tickled varied.

When my back portion is tickled, a smooth and soothing ticklish sensation is felt that drives me for the pleasure of sex. However, on tickling around my abdomen area and lower hip portion, I feel so ticklish that I cannot move my legs as it seems that my lower portion has become inactive with the activation of sexual pleasure. Moreover, during sex, if the breast and the bikini area are tickled then the intensity of sex increases thus making the sexual experience better.

My erogenous zones are ears, neck, breasts, my back, and I enjoy being touched, kissed, licked there. I laugh, I wiggle, I like it, I enjoy it.

During sex I like him to tickle my soft bums and down to the back of my knees. It takes me to cloud nine which means good, pleasurable and to die for orgasm!

My inner thighs and back are the right spots to tickle during foreplay.

To be super sensitive to tickling and I completely enjoy it. I indeed laugh out naturally while he tickles me during the act- the reason being a combined reaction of getting tickled and the pleasure of sex.

Behind my ears, my toes, my butt, my belly button, are all places I like to be tickled during sex and I enjoy every bit of it.

Tickles on my ribs don't make me sexual but, on my lap, or around my neck or my stomach and butt area makes me feel so.

About being tickled in the butt. Personally, I have felt that it is more prone to being ticklish, when my partner tries to even simply touch there or do any other crazy stuff there. I feel like that area is more ticklish as it is something I am usually shy about, hence adds to the sensation of being tickled.

One woman wanted her tickling organized like fine dining.

Tickling is the best way to set up the mood of my partner and mine as well. We always start from tickling each other's ears and neck. The tickling on the neck is a huge turn on that always work and leads to a perfect sexual experience. Slowly my partner would start to tickle me and tease me by touching my tits, my stomach, naval using the soft touch of fingers. These tickling experiences are the best experiences. I also enjoy the tickling experiences on my back. Before penetration my partner would always tickle my inner thighs and at that very moment it feels so good.

In some cases, the sites are chosen by her partner.

So, for imitating my tickling approach, my partner used to randomly tickle me romantically during our sex breaks. Particularly he tickles me on my neck, where I have a black mole which is quite attractive, underneath my boobs and also on my belly button. In all these body parts, when I am tickled, I feel comfortable and less conscious as I am with my partner since we both enjoy the phase. Hence, I think it's these body parts when being tickled during sex,

My breast, my armpit, my navel, stomach, butt, and lap. These are the areas he tickles me during sex.

Although the women reported many parts of the body as being erotic and sensitive to tickling, the breasts, specifically the nipples, stood out as a favorite.

Role of tickling in sex — little tingles and gentle tickling definitely help during sex and sensitizes parts of your body. Talking about the role of laugh inducing tickles during sex — The most tickle sensitive part on my body are my nipples, so much so that even gentle touches make me wiggle and squirm. These wiggles and squirms are such that I always end up burying my face in my partner's chest.

During sex, my partner tickles my boobs to get me awake for more sex, and I do enjoy it rather than being pissed. I do find it interesting, sexual and energetic when the tickling happens in the naked body. Each time he wanted to wake me to have extended sex, he used to grab and tickle my boobs.

Multitasking during sex, by stimulating my genitals at the same time tickling my boobs have been the best part.

During sex, I have been tickled on my boobs the most, especially the nipple area, which has always aroused me as well as my partner in the act. I indeed laugh out naturally while he tickles me during the act—the reason being a combined reaction of getting tickled and the pleasure of sex. Also, the way my nipples erect while being tickled has been interesting to both of us. The next most frequently tickled part during sex is my belly button, which also seems to be super sensitive to tickling, and I completely enjoy it.

Tickling my nipples gives me the shivers, in a good way.

Some women preferred to be tickled in their most sexually sensitive areas.

I like being tickled around the private and sensitive parts of my body by my lover or spouse as it gives me immense pleasure and the urge to do sex with my lover or spouse.

When my partner tickled me to improve my mood, I felt tremendously ticklish in the private parts of my body where I received the tickle and instantly my mood improved with the desire for doing sex with my partner. The feeling of ticklish that is generated by getting tickled by my partner around the private parts of the body gives me an immense pleasure of sex and that drives me to the soothness of heaven.

There's this stronger feeling I get when I'm being tickled before sex, especially in my vagina area. It makes sex more interesting and stronger. I don't know how to explain this.

In contrast, there were also others who preferred not to be tickled in sexually sensitive areas.

Tickling often sexually arouses me, especially in the non-genital area. While genital tickling is too forward and direct, tickling the surrounding areas like inner thighs or hips gives a flair of expectation, teasing and edging. If I'm close to orgasm, tickling on the neck will make it happen faster (not necessarily more intense, but faster).

During sex my neck become more ticklish and more like erogenous zone. When he saw me react in that way, I told him to do it again next time for better mood on my part. It made me laugh a lot (but not too much). If I do not express it by that it is less of an experience added with wiggles (body reaction) and it helps me get in the mood.

There were 171 women who answered an open-ended question about where they were tickled during sex. A number of women reported more than one place. The three places most often reported were the breast or nipples (71%), neck (66%), and sides (41%).

The Percentage of Women Who Listed a Particular Place as Tickled During Sex (N=171)	
Breast or nipples	72%
Neck	66%
Nipples	47%
Sides	41%
Breast	32%
Thighs	31%
Belly or navel	29%
Back	28%
Vulva	25%
Underarm	16%
Butt	12%
Ear	10%
Feet	8%
Waist	5%
Knees	4%
Perineum	4%
Hip	2%

UNPLEASANT TICKLING

Of course, there is more to tickling than laughs and giggles; there can be considerable unpleasantness. The common reasons women don't like being tickled are described below.

VIOLATION OF PERSONAL SPACE

Don't like at all because I just don't like anybody touching my body and making me feel uncomfortable.

I have never been ticklish, but I have always been averse to people touching me. If people tickled me on my skin, it was just a sensation of discomfort.

Over the years, I have been very vocal about my issue with tickling and the word consent means more to me now than it ever did. I try my best to communicate that I am not the person who will give a good reaction when tickled. And because of my childhood and growing-up experiences with tickling, I have developed a fear that in my mind is worse than being in the same room with a spider or lizard.

My body's reaction to tickling has always been extreme. The mere indication of someone approaching me can cause me to feel uncomfortable and unsettled in my skin. There is no sense of excitement and joy when it comes to being tickled. Instead, there is huge terror in being approached by different individuals who have no respect for your body's privacy.

I generally hate tickling. I consider intrusive and an overstepping of the boundaries of personal space. I need to give specific consent to get tickled. Otherwise, I get angry with people that suddenly feel the urge to tickle me.

UNPLEASANT SENSATION

Because it is irritating. I start feeling pain in my body when I fail to control laugh caused by tickling.

I feel uncomfortable and irritated when anyone tickles me. It's not because the other person is making me uncomfortable or something. But getting tickled is not my thing.

I (personally) don't like to be tickled anywhere on my body because I'm too sensitive and I feel uncomfortable and irritated when anyone tickles me.

It was almost always painful, not pleasurable.

I didn't like it, even though my body jerked. I had to force a smile in place of resentment.

I hate the feeling I get when I'm tickled.

LOSS OF CONTROL

My least favorite places to be tickled give me a feeling of a loss of control and I simply want it to stop. The more it lasts, the more uncomfortable I am.

The other type of bad experience is related to situations when my partner tickles me for longer than a few seconds and in a position where I am unable to stop him or move away – at that point I feel I have no control over the twitching, laughing and my body in general. I am not entirely sure why this feels so upsetting, but I feel it is related to the feeling of powerlessness and inability to defend myself, even though my partner never hurt me and was never aggressive in any way

Tickling has always made me feel like I am helpless and under attack. There is no escape, and I hate feeling like that. It makes me extremely anxious, and I often get panic attacks. It makes my heart race and gives a negative feeling all over my body, which often leads to goosebumps.

LASTS TOO LONG

Some women found that, even if tickling is not an unpleasant sensation at the beginning, it can quickly become so.

For me, tickling is an extremely uncomfortable touch, it discomforts me and causes slight anger even when I am tickled only out of love. The sensation caused by it brings a stimulation of delight for the first few seconds only, but then the feeling changes adversely and needs to be stopped right away.

I must say though, while I am delighted by the prospect of him tickling me, I don't enjoy it when he does so continuously. After a few moments, it starts to feel itchy.

SOCIALLY INAPPROPRIATE RESPONSES

Some women were most upset by their socially inappropriate response to tickling.

I can never let anyone tickle me. It's kind of embarrassing.

I hate being tickled. I can't help but that throaty big laughter with all my teeth on display is out and my body is going in repulsive fits and jerks.

It was from some of my friends I learned that the boys tickle or touch us girls to see how susceptible we are to a sexual stimulus (this, however, is very true to some extent). The more positively we react to their tickling the more sexually vulnerable we look to them. It is for this same reason that I had to learn to control how I react to tickles.

DISTURBING PHYSIOLOGICAL RESPONSES

Even if the tickling sensation itself is not unpleasant, the physiological responses it causes may be.

I was so absorbed in tickling my brother that I didn't notice that my family was creeping up to tickle me. I almost died that evening, they rushed to get my inhaler. I was laughing so hard that it became difficult to breathe, I had asthma.

Every time he tickles, I laugh out loud and can't breathe at all. After that I will cough all the time.

I could not breathe. I felt helpless, out of control. It's like I was falling and there was no one who would catch me. I was an outsider in my own body.

Severe sensations of panic, anxiety, and loss of control can also occur from tickling.

It always felt like I was being attacked, even though it wasn't actually hurting me. I just felt how my body would reject the tickling; it seemed overpowering, and I would enter into a state of panic.

I often read that tickling was used as torture for people for ages, and I can relate to it like no other. My memories of being a young child and being tortured by my siblings, cousins, random uncles, and dad tickled me unmercifully whenever they could. I can still remember the sensation of helplessness and desperation, wanting to cry, scream, and get away while they laughed at me.

I want nothing more than for the tickling to stop, but I have no way of communicating this other than through my words. From the tickler's point of view, however, these words seem to be contradicted by the more immediate and primal reaction of laughter. I can understand why ticklers feel that there can't be much harm in it, but to me, it is an awful and victimizing experience. It leaves

*me feeling frustrated, helpless, and angry at myself for my own
inability to communicate my needs effectively.*

*When I'm tickled, I feel as though every muscle in my body freezes.
My arms and legs try to fight, but sometimes they too, become
motionless. The act of being tickled leaves me feeling trapped, and
helpless. Although the first few seconds I may release a giggle or
two, I begin to hold my breath as a result of feeling unable to move,
or escape. This puts my body into further panic — I'm unable to
move OR breathe; it's terrifying.*

In one account, the woman described a combination of anxiety
and pleasure.

*Many of the sensations that I feel are felt by my friends: anxiety
that slowly builds as you twist and squirm trying to get away, a
feeling of pleasure or happiness that results in laughing, a quick
burst of energy and wakefulness, and a loss of physical and emotional control which makes you vulnerable.*

Even though the reasons for disliking tickling are common
and strong, the previous results show that they are not universally shared.

ABUSIVE TICKLING

Although tickling is often unpleasant, abusive tickling–sometimes intentionally and sometimes not–is worse than unpleasant.
It can do long-term psychological damage.

Tickling Torture

The use of tickling for torture is well known. It was primarily used against political prisoners, blasphemers, or heretics as a means of psychological torment. Tickling torture typically involves immobilizing the victim and tickling them in sensitive areas to inflict agony through prolonged tickling sessions that could last for hours or days and result in long-lasting trauma. Tickling as a form of torture has been widely condemned as a violation of human rights.

However, tickle torture is not confined to the distant past. One Indian woman reported the tickle torture of her grandfather in the war against Pakistan and how he suffered severe psychological effects from these experiences.

> *My grandfather recalled the day he went into complete shock when both of them were sleeping in their prison cell, that is when three enemy soldiers dragged him out of the cellar and tied him to a chair, naked. One of them told the other to take out the feather from his pocket; the other fellow followed his order. They started to tickle him in his armpits, his feet, and all sorts of other private places. They believed it to be some tickle-torture modern method.*

No other participants reported anything nearly as severe, but they did share accounts of being intentionally tortured by siblings and classmates.

> *Well, I didn't exactly find my happy place through tickling. At the age of 12, my oldest brother tickled on me as a way of torture, until*

I cried, until I peed on myself, until he was bored and found some other thing to do, or other butterfly to hunt.

One girl was tickled ruthlessly by other students for being the daughter of the principal.

The guys hinted at each other and began tickling me, as though for fun, but I was not comfortable at all. I could hear them murmuring in anger that they wanted to hurt me some way or the other. This incident had a huge impact on my life and also became a reason why I wanted to shift to a girls-only college for my graduation.

Both siblings and parents used it as a weapon for control or punishment.

As a child I was very, very ticklish and my older sister used to use this against me to get me to do things for her. I have clear memories of being stuck on my back on the floor with my sister attacking me with tickles under my arms and my feet until I screamed and agreed to do her chores for her.

My mother would get relatives to tickle me so as to put a black soap, locally known as Ghana soap, in my private parts, which would be unbearable and very uncomfortable throughout the day. My mom also tickles me after spanking; she would throw me up and tickle my stomach till she's sure that tears have stopped rolling down my eyes.

I remember when I would not listen to my parents or didn't do what my older siblings would tell me to, they'd threaten to tickle me. That might seem funny to some, but it was just about the worst thing that could happen to me.

No doubt one of the reasons for its common use for control and punishment is that is easy to deny the harm of tickling.

I remember my mother would always lecture me on how I didn't have to react this way and that it was okay.

Tickling as Inappropriate Behavior

Even a one-time experience not intended to cause physical or psychological pain could be a traumatic, life-changing event.

Talking about my worst experience of being tickled, I am a national level swimmer and was trained in the swimming pool at the high school campus. I was in the swimsuit, resting by the gallery, and he came up to me. He pretended to console me, and abruptly, tickled me on my armpits, which I did not like at all. That was my last day of coaching just because of this indecent act of his.

The trauma of gang tickling was mentioned by several women.

I will never forget this one incident that took place on my 17th birthday. All my friends came to my party and with them came this male friend of mine who was pretty normal at school. I don't know what got into him when we all were playing tag. He not only tagged me, but he started tickling me. After screaming and cussing at him, he still wouldn't stop, and that's when everyone else joined him. 'Let's tickle the birthday girl' — it was like my worst nightmare was coming to life,

Other times, the trauma was caused by repeated offenses.

When I was about eight years old, and my brothers would do it to bother me. It always felt like I was being attacked, The tickling seemed overpowering, and I would enter into a state of panic. Afterwards, whatever little movement my brothers made would make me jump back, panicked of being tickled again.

Tickling intended to be playful becomes abusive if it lasts too long. Some women even reported losing consciousness, which can happen from hyperventilation or overstimulation of the vagus nerve.

We were playing a game, where one tickles the other. So we tickled each other and laughed our hearts out, I remember laughing so hard and telling my siblings to stop it; however, they were enjoying the laughter. I kept laughing till I had no more energy left. I think I passed out and peed on myself. I must have woken up after some minutes to the sight of worried siblings.

I was usually tickled till I had to beg for my life, to be spared because I could feel myself losing consciousness and I have passed out a few times from being tickled. I don't wish this experience on even my greatest enemy.

The examples above are serious offenses with long-term consequences. No doubt, the torturer was ignorant in some cases but didn't care in others. Given the inherent meanness of our species, it's not clear whether education about tickling abuse would lead to more or less abuse.

Effect of Abuse on Attitudes Toward Tickling

Our data showed that bad experiences as a child might influence adult attitudes toward being tickled. Of 31 participants who had been affected by bad experiences with tickling as a child, only five (16%) sometimes liked being tickled.

Bad Experiences with Being Tickled as a Child Predicted Adult Reaction to Tickling		N	Sometimes Pleasant
Affected by bad experiences with tickling	Possibly	31	16%
	No	181	49%
All women		212	44%

It is also possible that women abused in childhood for any reason might not like tickling because liking tickling requires trust. However, we found that about the same percentage of abused and non-abused women sometimes found tickling pleasant (44%).

Childhood Abuse Did Not Predict Whether Women Found Tickling Pleasant		N	Sometimes Pleasant
Abuse	Possibly	99	43%
	No	113	44%
All participants		212	44%

WHY DID TICKLING EVOLVE?

All genes that are common in the population exist because, at some point, they helped our ancestors survive, reproduce, or both. Theoretically, the ancestors served by tickling could have been prehuman (nah) or tickling could have reached its fullest development for the purpose of helping humans (bingo). We begin this chapter with the ideas of why the participants thought tickling evolved and then discuss what our research findings suggest.

Our primary interest in this research was not the reason tickling evolved but its role in society. However, since the fundamentals of our personality and methods of interacting have not greatly changed, it is likely that its current and past roles are closely related.

WHAT PARTICIPANTS THOUGHT

We asked the participants whether they agreed with certain hypotheses about why they thought evolution caused people to become ticklish. Their responses are valuable to the extent they are more likely to choose hypotheses that fit with their personal experiences. No doubt, the responses of some women were influenced somewhat by what they learned from outside sources.

More than half of the participants, 57%, thought that tickling evolved because it had at least one of the following three sexual benefits: bonding with the opposite sex, enhancing sexual pleasure, or enhancing sexual attractiveness. Another 46% thought that it evolved because it improved bonding with children, and 35% because it improved bonding with friends. Thirty percent of the women also endorsed the hypothesis that tickling teaches children to protect their vulnerable areas. Only 21% of the participants endorsed the hypothesis that tickling was useful for providing an outlet for a type of fighting that did not cause damage.

The Percentage of 829 Participants Who Agree with Each Hypothesis for Why Evolution Caused People to Become Ticklish	
Hypotheses	
One or more sexual benefits	57%
To bond with the opposite sex	39%
To enhance sexual pleasure	32%
To enhance sexual attractiveness	28%
For parents to bond with children	46%
To bond with friends	35%
To teach children to protect their vulnerable areas	30%
To fight without doing damage	21%

EVOLUTIONARY HYPOTHESES SUPPORTED BY STUDY RESULTS

The study results and the participants' opinions supported the same three hypotheses: parent-child bonding, bonding with friends, and sexual benefits. That's not surprising because both the study results and the hypotheses chosen depended on the participants' experiences.

Many participants reported pleasure in tickling their children or fond memories of being tickled by their parents. From an evolutionary point of view, any trait that makes parents feel closer to their children will be selected for transmission because it improves childhood survival.

However, the persistence of ticklishness beyond infancy suggests that it also has value later in the life cycle. One post-infancy value is that it helps with bonding among friends and family members or even with creating new friendships.

The other post-infancy value is that it leads to more sex and longer sexual partnerships. Both written statements by the women and quantitative analysis of the data suggests that this is the primary driving force for the evolution of ticklishness. According to the written statements, tickling helped with the following:

1. Advancing relationships from hands-off to sexual
2. Increasing sexual arousal
3. Making women sexier by causing them to laugh and wiggle
4. Communicating sexual desire
5. Adding play to the relationship
6. Helping romantic partners recover from conflicts

The quantitative information supporting the importance of tickling in sexual relationships included the following:

1. Fifty-seven percent of the women thought that tickling was beneficial for bonding with the opposite sex, enhancing sexual pleasure, and/or enhancing sexual attractiveness.

2. Eighty-two percent of the women had been tickled by at least one of their dates, suggesting that many men find tickling sexually stimulating.

3. Since 54% of the women were tickled most often by their romantic partner, it is likely that a high percentage of the tickling occurs as part of a sexual relationship.

4. Many women liked tickling as part of their romantic relationships. In one data set, 56% liked being tickled by their romantic partner frequently or usually, and in another data set, 45% said that the first few seconds of being tickled by their lover felt good to them.

5. Forty-five percent of the women only accepted tickling from men they were involved with sexually: either dating or considering sex. This suggests that many women consider tickling an intimate act. Men given tickling rights are encouraged to continue their pursuits. Men denied those rights will use their courting energies more efficiently elsewhere.

6. There was also evidence that tickling was related to the husband's pleasure independently of the effect on the woman. More than 25% of the women said that they liked being tickled because it pleased their husbands. Other evidence is that sex was ruined by tickling more than rarely for 39% of the women. This suggests that tickling could be a pleasure for the male, even if it were negative for the woman.

All the benefits listed above not only promote reproduction but also help stabilize the relationship, which in turn helps the offspring survive. Although tickling in a sexual relationship does not benefit everyone, it must have benefited enough during the period of evolution so that a large percentage of the population became ticklish.

OTHER HYPOTHESES

There are other hypotheses than the three above for why people are ticklish. We will arbitrarily call these hypotheses false hypotheses. One of these is that ticklishness is a vestigial trait, meaning it may have served a purpose for ancestral species but is of no value to humans. An example of a vestigial trait is the appendix, which, until recently, was considered valuable only for providing surgical income. The vestigial hypothesis would be more convincing if humans were less ticklish than many other animals. Au contraire, tickling interactions are stronger and more complex in humans than in any other animal. Instead of a trait that is on the way out, tickling is a trait that clearly reached its peak in humans.

A second false hypothesis is widely cited on the internet and has scientific supporters who will take offense at our bah-humbug response to their ideas. That hypothesis is that ticklishness provides an evolutionary advantage by improving self-defense. The underlying assumption is that the most vulnerable areas of the body evolved to become ticklish to help people learn how to protect themselves. In addition, ticklish responses help individuals to be more responsive and alert to unexpected touches, enhancing their reflexes and defensive abilities.

The strongest argument for this hypothesis is that the most vulnerable area of the body, the neck, is often highly ticklish. Against this hypothesis is evidence from our study that the neck is also the body area where tickles are the most often pleasing. Also against this hypothesis is its inability to explain why the bottom of the foot is commonly very ticklish, why there is so much variation among people as to which spots are ticklish, and the total lack of evidence that ticklishness actually improves self-defense.

The ticklishness of areas poorly explained by the self-defense hypothesis makes more sense using the bonding hypothesis. For example, the ticklishness of the bottom of the foot can be explained because this part of the body is exposed only to those present during times when we are relaxing. The people we are with at that time are more likely to be those we want to bond with than to defend ourselves against. That's also true of under the arms. Other very ticklish sites, the neck, sides, and inner thighs are especially accessible during sex. The breast, nipple, and vulva are often ticklish. Touching them may have the dual purpose of making women laugh and increasing their arousal, both generally desirable to males.

EVOLUTIONARY ADVANTAGES OF UNPLEASANT TICKLING

If you were evolution, and you set out to create an all-purpose bonder, you would choose one that's always pleasant. However, evolution doesn't care about all-purpose bonders, it cares about what's in the long-term self-interest of the individual. That's why it created a bonder only with those most likely to help us, i.e., those we already feel close to or attracted to. It's not even a bonder with these people when they use it to interrupt our work or continue so long that it wastes a lot of our energy.

What's more difficult to explain is the severe unpleasantness of tickling. Why would there be a survival advantage to developing a trait that makes it easier for your brother or your enemy to torture you? One possibility is that it's better than the alternative. If torture was limited to methods that caused severe pain, the evil brother may do something that causes much longer-term physical damage than tickling does.

SUMMARY OF WHY TICKLISHNESS EVOLVED

1. Tickling increases bonding for some people in some relationships. Strong interpersonal bonds are critical assets for both survival and reproduction. Traits that promote these bonds will be selected by evolution.
2. Tickling enhances sexual experiences for some people. Better sexual experiences increase the likelihood of being selected as a mate and having a longer relationship with that mate. Longer relationships between parents improve the survival of their children.
3. Ticklishness enhances sexual attractiveness.
4. Acceptance of tickling may act as a gatekeeper that suggests whether a relationship is ready to move ahead. If a woman accepts tickling, her suitor may be encouraged; if

she doesn't, an unwelcome suitor may recognize the rejection before developing strong sexual expectations that may be managed in a more destructive way than in the earlier stages of a relationship.

TAKE AWAY MESSAGES

We presented extensive narrative information about personal experiences and statistical analyses of data collected using structured questionnaires. The narratives were rich in details and emotions. Your reactions might include 1) That is beyond my experience and fascinating. 2) She had experiences just like mine, or 3) Different women respond very differently to the same input.

The statistical analyses used quantitative information from hundreds of women to give a picture of aspects of the population that are intrinsically interesting, provide information about the importance of some behavior in society, give guidance about the acceptability of certain behaviors, and show relationships between certain characteristics that suggest directions for additional research.

We only indicated relationships if the findings met rigorous statistical criteria. However, some relationships were based on more participants than others, and some showed a dose/response relationship, i.e., the stronger the trait the more likely the woman would respond to tickling in a certain way. Larger sample sizes and dose responses relationships give us confidence that these relationships were not just strong in this dataset but will also be strong in numerous groups of women. The relationships reported below are those likely to be strong in numerous groups of women.

1. Of 1600 women, 54% were very ticklish or extremely ticklish. The percentages may be lower in the general population than in our study, but it's clear that many women are very ticklish, and tickling has the potential to influence their lives.
2. One-third of 919 women in the study had been tickled during the past week. This percentage varied little in different regions or cultures. There is no question that the desire to tickle is hard-baked into our genes.
3. More ticklish women were tickled more frequently, but less frequent tickling did not make women more or less ticklish.
4. There were enormous variations in responses to tickling: a) What one woman enjoyed, another hated, or the same woman hated under different conditions. b) The most ticklish spots for some women were not at all ticklish in others. c) Women responded very differently to tickling in different spots. d) The spots most preferred by some women were least liked by others.
5. More than 40% of ticklish women were glad they were ticklish.
6. Tickling sometimes improved bonding with children, friends, or lovers.
7. Forty-five percent of 152 women who were dating had been tickled in the past week compared to 24% of 198 women who were not in a romantic relationship. Clearly tickling is part of sexual interaction. Several women said that tickling facilitated physical intimacy.

8. Tickling is commonly used in foreplay. About 25% of women had better sex with tickling.

9. After puberty, tickling was an intimate interaction.

10. The norms for who is allowed to tickle us and who we are allowed to tickle are similar across diverse societies. There are good reasons for these norms, and problems are caused by ignoring them.

11. A number of personality traits are more common in ticklish women, especially nervousness and enjoying sex. Women who liked taking risks or were happier were also more ticklish. These traits may make women more sensitive or less resistant to tickling, or they may be influenced by the same brain wiring that influences ticklishness.

12. Personality traits associated with the enjoyment of tickling included being more ticklish, liking caresses, liking sex, and liking risk. Finding the reasons for these associations will improve our understanding of why different women respond so differently to tickling.

We hope that this study will improve the understanding of tickling, make it a more acceptable topic of conversation, and stimulate further research.

APPENDIX: INTO THE RESEARCH WEEDS

The study was self-financed, which was a hardship, but it had the benefit of eliminating all bureaucracy except what we self-imposed to make certain that no participants were negatively affected by the study.

PARTICIPANTS AND DATA COLLECTION

To find participants, we hired women freelancers from online agencies to ask their female friends and family members over the age of 18 to participate. Only women were studied for three reasons:

1. The researchers had limited time and money, so any effort spent studying men would have reduced the information from women.
2. Women are easier to recruit because they have more social networks and are generally less ashamed of being ticklish.
3. Women are more likely to be tickled than men and are more often tickled against their will, making them better sources regarding both the positive and negative aspects of being tickled.

THE QUESTIONNAIRES

All information analyzed came from responses to questionnaires. Initially, we used only structured questionnaires that had specific questions and short or predefined response options. Questions were asked about the following topics:

1. Demographics (e.g., country, age, marital status)
2. Physical responses to tickling (ticklishness overall and in specific places, laughing, and wiggling)
3. Psychological responses to tickling (e.g., their feeling about being tickled and how it affected their relationships)
4. Tickling interactions (e.g., frequency of being tickled, who does the tickling)
5. Personality characteristics (e.g., liking to win, liking sex, etc.)
6. Life experiences (e.g., childhood abuse)

There were five very different structured questionnaires. The questions came from those commonly used in epidemiological studies or psychological tests, what we found on the internet about tickling, and ideas from participants. Each questionnaire had a different set of questions, but many questions were on more than one of these questionnaires. Each of the five questionnaires also had slightly different versions because a few questions were added after some participants had already completed the first version. In addition to the English version of each questionnaire, there were also versions in Spanish, Croatian, or Arabic for three of the questionnaires. There was also a very short questionnaire used as the beginning of the study.

LONG NARRATIVE ANSWERS

In addition to the five structured questionnaires, some questionnaires only included general questions that requested long answers in essay form. Answers to these questions provided insight into the findings derived from statistical analyses and made the information we received more relatable. In almost all cases, the essays were from individual women, but in a few cases, they were reports by a recruiter of a discussion of several women. There were 198 responses from individual women or groups of women to essay questions.

Some women who wrote these essays were not native English speakers. If their answers were not clear, we did not include them in our reports. We corrected grammatical errors only if it were necessary to facilitate rapid reading. In a few cases, we summarized text that was too long or too sexual for a general audience.

PERSONALITY TRAITS STUDIED

We studied whether various psychological characteristics were predictive of ticklishness or of liking to be tickled. The characteristics were chosen based on our own ideas, the ideas of participants, or the characteristics of standard instruments to measure psychological characteristics. We put the characteristics in groups to help us organize the presentation. It's unlikely that anyone else would use a similar grouping to the one that we did. Fortunately for us, our bizarre grouping has no implications for how the results are interpreted.

Many of the characteristics were only evaluated by questionnaires that we developed at the end of the study. Therefore, these characteristics were not evaluated in as many participants as other characteristics.

Personality Traits Studied	
Group name	Traits within group
Attitude to physical contact:	dislike light touch, enjoy sex, like caresses, like hugs
Sociability	dislike being in crowds, extroverted, helpful to strangers, likable, kind, tolerant, try to please
Assertiveness:	dislike criticism, like winning, confident, fear control
Acceptance of risk:	like risk, like security,
Psychological health	happy, past abuse, past trauma, underappreciated, worry,
Intellectual:	analytical, creative, dislike routines, organized, perfectionist
Physiology:	dislike bright lights, dislike loud sounds, dislike loud voices dislike scratchy clothing, energetic, ignore pain, nervous

NUMBERS OF RESPONDENTS

There were 2076 structured questionnaires completed from 43 countries. These questionnaires do not include about 400 questionnaires that were completed a second time to check for the reliability of the answers.

Of the 2076 structured questionnaires completed, 1361 provided email addresses. By using these emails, we were able to determine that only 45 women, 3.4% (45/1316 total women) of the women who completed two questionnaires. All 715 women who did not provide email addresses answered the first questionnaire before there was a request for an email address. Few, if any, of the recruiters of these 715 women also recruited women for later studies. Therefore, the percentage of women who completed more than one questionnaire was less than 3.4.% Although no amount of duplicate data is kosher, this level will have zero impact on the study results.

In our analyses, we tabulated the number of specific answers to our questions. In some cases the actual number of participants may be slightly smaller than the number of questionnaires that are tabulated. However, we refer to the tabulated number as the number of participants because the study is about participants, not about questionnaires, and the numbers are almost the same.

There were more than 200 women who wrote long narrative answers. We don't know the exact number because in a few cases, the recruiter interviewed a group of women and compiled the results. Some women who wrote essays had not completed structured questionnaires and some were not from countries that completed any structured questionnaires. The countries with at least nine persons who wrote essays were Nigeria, India, the USA, and Pakistan.

VARIATION IN NUMBERS FOR EACH QUESTION

The tabulated data in this study is based on responses to one or more questions from the structured questionnaires. The number of participants who answered a given question or combination of questions varies greatly for the following reasons: 1) Some participants advertently or inadvertently skipped a specific question that they should have answered, . 2) Many questions were on more than one questionnaire. Therefore, there were more participants who answered the questions that were in common. 3) Some questions on different questionnaires were similar enough that they could be combined for some analyses but not others.

You will be forgiven if you're now thinking that this study wasn't classy, i.e., carefully planned in advance. Instead of staying with the plan as classy researchers do, we changed questions depending on what additional information we thought would be valuable based on our findings up to that time.

CHARACTERISTICS OF THE PARTICIPANTS

The tables below report data only on women who completed the structured questionnaires. Seventeen of these countries had more than 20 questionnaires. There were about 2025 women who completed 2076 questionnaires.

The Number of Participants from Each Country					
Country	N*	Country	N*	Country	N*
Algeria	27	Mexico	198	Spain	31
Australia	12	Montenegro	18	Sri Lanka	18
Bangladesh	12	Nepal	19	Turkey	59
Brazil	21	Nigeria	181	Ukraine	39
Croatia	31	Pakistan	74	USA	87
India	688	Philippines	130	Venezuela	54
Kenya	77	Romania	78	Other ‡	54
Kosovo	25	Serbia	143	Total	2076

Participants in countries that may have cultural similarities were grouped together as shown in the following table.

Number of Participants in Each Group Who Completed Structured Questionnaires		
Group	N	Countries in the region
Africa	262	Ghana, Kenya, Nigeria
Asia	859	India, Nepal, Singapore, Sri Lanka
English culture	115	Australia, Canada, New Zealand, White South African, USA, UK
Europe	380	Albania, Belgium, Belarus, Bosnia, Croatia, France, Germany, Italy, Kosovo, Montenegro, Romania, Serbia, Spain, Sweden, Ukraine
Latin America	277	Argentina, Brazil, Dominican Republic, Mexico, Venezuela
Muslim	183	Algeria, Bangladesh, Egypt, Iran, Oman, Pakistan, Saudi Arabia, Turkey
All women	2076	

Age

Most women in this study were young; only 10% were older than 45. One reason for the young age is that many of the recruiters were women in their 20s looking for part-time work, and these women recruited their friends. A second reason was that younger women were more willing to complete these questionnaires. Although the participants were younger than the general population, they do represent the age when tickling has the greatest role and is most important to study.

The Percentage of Participants in Each Age Range (N =2015)	
Age range	% Of total
18-25	34%
26-35	39%
36-45	17%
46-60	8%
Over 60	2%

Relationships

Nearly 40% of the women were married. Only 26% were not in any romantic relationship. In one data set of 407 women, more than 90% had experienced intercourse and therefore could have experienced tickling as part of sexual interactions. This suggests that a high percentage of the women in this study could comment accurately on the role of tickling in romantic relationships.

The Percentage of Participants in Each Relationship Category (N = 2045)	
Relationship	% Of total
Married	40%
Committed	18%
Dating	16%
No current	26%

Sexual Orientation

Eighty-eight percent of the women were exclusively heterosexual. Twice as many women who were not exclusively heterosexual were attracted to men and women as to women alone, which is similar to percentages found in other studies.

Romantic Partners (N =977)	
Men	88%
Women	4%
Both	8%

WAS THE STUDY ANY GOOD?

We think so for the following reasons:

1. We have considerable background doing high-quality, population-based research.
2. We spent four years thoughtfully and carefully conducting this research.
3. The recruiters were generally enthusiastic about the study.
4. Data managers kept the data organized.
5. We confirmed the reliability of the participant responses. These results are not presented in this book. Although there were participants who gave different answers to the same question at different times or gave inconsistent answers to related questions, we believe that the quality of the data was accurate enough to be useful. Our reasons for this belief are we knew for certain many women were committed to accurate responses, results were consistent across recruiters, many results were expected, and the most surprising results were confirmed in different data sets.
6. We used universally accepted statistical methods to determine which relationships did not occur by chance, and we only reported relationships that had less than one chance in a thousand of occurring by chance. Only after that did we make decisions about how to present the data in an understandable manner.
7. We did not manipulate in any way the questionnaires, the data, or the analyses to get the results we wanted.

Another positive aspect of this research is that it included participants who varied greatly with respect to every demographic imaginable: country, culture, ethnicity, religion, job, education, income, and type of community. More than 17 countries were included in the research, and even within one country especially India, the country with the highest number of recruits, there was enormous variation in the participants with respect to all demographic characteristics. This diversity makes us confident that most results apply to many types of women regardless of their culture or geographical location.

A weakness of the study is that we could not be sure what caused differences between countries or groups of countries. The causes may have been genetic or cultural differences between countries, but they also may have been caused by different approaches used by recruiters in different countries. If this did happen, it should not have had a large effect because many different recruiters were involved for each group of countries.

There is even less likelihood that inconsistencies in the administration of the questionnaires could have created relationships that did not involve nationality. Any unsystematic errors in our study are more likely to obscure important relationships than to cause apparent relationships that didn't really exist. Therefore, we expect our findings to be replicated in better studies conducted in the future. For example, the association found between ticklishness and liking sex is almost certainly not explained by flaws in the study.

Of course, the validity of our results can only be confirmed by other studies. The gold standard study would use sophisticated methods to select participants and train research assistants to follow the same protocol for administering the questionnaire. It would also use the results of our study to improve the questions we had.

We have no shame in recognizing that future studies will do a better job than we did. In fact, one goal of this study is to show that the topic is interesting enough to motivate other researchers to do a better job. Our most important goal was to provide interesting and valid information to our readers.